To my
friend MIKE!

[signature]

FRMED

FRMED

A Journey of
Spiritual Formation

R. Kent Smith

Formed: A Journey of Spiritual Formation

Copyright © 2022
R. Kent Smith

Unless otherwise noted, all Scripture quotations herein are from the Authorized King James Version of the Bible.

ISBN 978-0-578-38370-5

FOR INFORMATION CONTACT:
R. Kent Smith
rks@conroeupc.org

To My Lady Tracie

This journey
My journey
Our journey
would have been incomplete alone.

"Welcome to My World"

Special thanks to
My Mentors of Mastery:
Marcus, Ralph, and Ken

You awakened me!

Contents

Introduction

I did not like or appreciate having the question presented to me. After all, I am a successful pastor and leader with more than four decades of leadership and pastoral experience. I rather enjoy asking hard questions but quite honestly did not appreciate the question my mentor asked me. It bothered me. I was intimidated by it. I could not immediately form a reply. So I pondered my answer over a few days.

Three days later I wrote three sentences to answer the offending question. Finally, four days later I summoned the courage to read aloud the simple responses I had formed. As I read, I felt the liberation of overcoming personal vulnerabilities. To date I have shared those three sentences with scores of others. While we visit through this book, you will learn the results of this soul-searching.

This treatise is about me. I know this sounds a bit self-declarative, but my assignment in pursuit of a master's degree included a self-assessment of my journey of spiritual formation. An assessment of myself cannot be complete without my analyzing and communicating about myself. Thus, my task requires me to talk about me.

Such a discussion mandates honesty, self-awareness, integrity, and vulnerability. The task also requires an overview of my past, present, and future. I will discuss where and how God has led me—where He brought me from and how He has and continues to use me. Most importantly, I will assess the outcome God has planned for me, what He has been forming in me, and why and where He has chosen to lead my journey of spiritual formation. This work is not intended to research new and deep ideas, but I submit my evaluation of my journey.

None of us have arrived, but somehow, we all are here. *The Message* transliteration says it this way:

> *I'm not saying that I have this all together, that I have it made. But I am well on my way, reaching out for Christ, who has so wondrously reached out for me. Friends, don't get me wrong: By no means do I count myself an expert in all of this, but I've got my eye on the goal, where God is beckoning us onward—to Jesus* (Philippians 3:12-13).

Since this is my self-assessment, let me continue in this version of Philippians for another two verses.

> *I'm off and running, and I'm not turning back. So let's keep focused on that goal, those of us who want everything God has for us* (Philippians 3:14-15).

Therefore, like Paul I am off and running, not turning back. I intend to stay focused and to allow God to finish His work of spiritual formation in my life.

Formative Foundations

The book of beginnings opens, "In the beginning God created the heaven and the earth." This declarative occasion stands firm in time as the first recorded moment and affirms the reality of God and His creative plan for the heavens and the earth. For five and one-half creative days God created. He created heavens, earth, land, sea, day, night, stars, moon, sun, water, firmaments, plants, seeds, herbs, fruit, animals, fish, birds, and all the rest of His beautiful creation that we call our earth and environment. On the sixth day, according to His preordained design, He determined to make a man in His likeness. Straightway He created the first man, Adam, in His own image.

The second chapter of Genesis resumes the narrative with a bit more explanation. After the first day of rest, God chose to iterate a bit of what He had done in those first six days. He reminded us that all His creation had come from His creative word, but man was different. God formed man from the dust of the ground. God got His hands dirty with man. Man came from the created things God had spoken into existence. God then breathed His breath of life into the nostrils of His newly formed creation.

Man was formed from the elements God had created. The breath of God had been breathed into his nostrils. In this record, we learn that the first man, Adam, and every other man since has the created dirt of this world in his flesh and the breath of God's world in him at the same time. Every man has a living, eternal soul. Consider this event as an equation in mathematical terms.

A formed man + the breath of God = a living soul

It becomes clear that the Creator of the beginnings took time and deliberation in the formation of man. God continues His process of formation in each of us. Spiritual formation is God's process.

Abraham's formative process set him upon a journey, looking for that city whose builder and maker is God. It led him from Ur of the Chaldees to Egypt, the plains of Sodom, and the sacrificial mountain of Moriah.

Isaac's formation caused him to remain a wanderer, who cleaned out his father's wells. He also learned he had to dig his own wells.

Jacob went through the heat and fire of formation with deceit and exile from his home for a near lifetime. The formation of his son, Joseph, looked like it would be different. The favored child of the favorite wife, He dreamed outlandish dreams. His formation led him to the pit, Potiphar's house, prison, and the palace. He was betrayed and falsely accused, but eventually he was governor. Then his dreams came to fulfillment.

Three Hebrew young men, captives in a foreign land, discovered that they might have to go through the fire of persecution. Nonetheless, the trial was simply part of God's formative process for their lives.

A man born blind walked in a dark world his entire lifetime until the day our Lord smeared creative mud into his eyes and sent him to wash them. Jesus explained that there was purpose in his blindness. How can blindness be the purpose and plan of God? God said the purpose of the man's lifetime handicap was the glorification of the Son of Man!

From the sixth day of Creation until today, formation is God's process. There are no shortcuts. It takes time and is on God's timetable. It requires God's time and not man's.

The requirements for the Old Testament priesthood stated that a man had to be thirty years of age to minister in the Temple. While no doubt many men might have been ministerially qualified earlier, God's plan gave time for His formative process in the aspiring priest. The apostle Paul would parallel this teaching by saying that no minister should be a novice, one who has not experienced the proving ground of God's formative processes.

Personal Formative Foundations

My formative foundations are broad and deep. A bit of family history illustrates this background.

On New Year's Eve 1899, a group of students gathered in Topeka, Kansas, to pray for the Holy Ghost to be given them in the same fashion as on the Day of Pentecost. That night, the dawn of a new century was also the rebirth of an era of spiritual formation. The fire of the Holy Ghost fell upon those students and soon spread to Houston, Texas. Along the banks of Buffalo Bayou, tents were raised, and the message of this "new thing" was preached. Thousands received the infilling of the Holy Ghost.

From those initial outpourings, men preached with great fervor the message of the new birth. The message of Pentecost spread quickly east and north into the East Texas areas, and throughout the 1920s men preached in tents, brush arbors, living rooms, trains, and street corners. Churches were formed that are still in operation.

In the mid-1920s in Bronson, Texas, Lee's family of four brothers and his parents came to a meeting and were filled with the Holy Ghost. Lee would later meet Leola at a gospel assembly, and they would fall in love and marry. Lee and Leola settled to raise their family in Rosevine, Texas, where Lee began preaching to the community.

Lee established and built a church with his personal funds. He donated land and had a new building erected, but in a tragic turn of events, the church burned to the ground.

Lee rebuilt the church, and Rosevine United Pentecostal Church has ministered to the needs of the local community for more than eighty years.

Meanwhile, in Pelly, Texas, revival fires burned. As a great church was growing, a board member took offense at the ministry of the pastor. The official collected the pastor's possessions from the church and parsonage, placed them on the street, and literally threw the pastor out.

Fred and Lois had come to know the Lord only a few months prior. They loved their pastor and helped him to find a place for his things. The next Sunday the pastor held a service in the living room of Fred and Lois's house; the next week a church was organized that exists today. Peace Tabernacle United Pentecostal Church has been in full operation since late 1939.

Both families were deeply involved for their lifetimes in kingdom work. Fred and Lois's youngest child was named Ronnie. Lee and Leola's youngest was Joye. Ronnie and Joye met while attending the first youth camp on the Pentecostal campgrounds in Lufkin, Texas. They were married in 1960 and soon gave birth to a bouncing baby boy named Kent. I am he.

My parents were old-time Pentecostal leaders. Dad preached hell is hot and heaven is high. He taught us things were either right or wrong. Compromise of biblical doctrine could not be tolerated. Lifestyle decisions had consequences. We went to church regardless of sickness or homework.

He taught me to pray. He taught me to preach. He taught me to give. He taught me to sacrifice. He taught me to put everything on the line for the kingdom of God. He put me in the position of song-service leader—whatever happened to song service?—when I reached the age of twelve. When I had normal teenage missteps, he sat me down for weeks, and the church people would ask, "What did you do this time?"

Shortly after Tracie and I married, I asked him to loan me two hundred dollars for an insurance deductible for two days. He refused, saying, "Son, I raised you to be a man." That was forty years ago, and I have never asked again.

Dad often apologizes to me for the way he raised me, but I never accept those apologies. The actions and requirements he placed on me were both parental and spiritually formative directions I would not have learned without him. For me there is no greater spiritual giant than my father.

He has retired from pastoring several times. Even in the twilight years of his life, he still holds the respect of many. He has been gifted as a confidant to leaders who have needed a firm yet gentle hand upon them. Dad turned eighty this year, and I know our time is limited. His health is failing, his steps are uncertain, his hearing about gone—though he does not admit any of this—but his anointing continues as God uses him to help the formation of other ministers.

Such is the process of spiritual formation. Such formation is a journey. For generations my family on both sides has given, sacrificed, preached, prayed, rejoiced, and even wept during the process of God's work in our lives.

Tracie and I met at Texas Bible College when our fathers were students. She was five and I was seven. After our marriage in 1982, we began our own spiritual journey. Ours has been a journey of constant formation. God has long-term plans, and even at my sixty-year mark, God continues to work His processes in our lives and my ministry.

We have endeavored many kinds of ministry, not all of which were successful. For example, one year I was between assistant-pastor positions. I decided that I would make a great traveling evangelist. I can confidently attest that I, R. Kent Smith, hold the world's record for the worst traveling evangelist ever! But that painful year was also part of God's formative process in our lives.

Friction creates the best pearls. Heat creates the best diamonds, and God's fiery process of formation creates the best men. It takes both friction and a man to polish a pearl. It takes friction, pressure, fiery trials, God, and other men to complete the spiritual formation in us.

John Mark was an early failure and a disappointment to the apostle Paul. Paul in his frustration would banish the young man from the ministry team. Years later Paul wrote to Timothy and instructed him to bring John Mark with him when he came to Rome. Paul declared that now John Mark was profitable to the ministry. God's formative process for John Mark appears to have been a bit bumpy, but when the timing was right and God's formation was complete, the door of opportunity opened for him. Imagine John Mark's excitement when he got the "email" from Luke that Paul wanted him to come back to join the ministry team!

God's formation of my life and ministry has included near bankruptcy, long and lonely years, misunderstandings, false accusations, lies, an unwed pregnant daughter, a granddaughter drowning at the age of fifteen months in my front yard, and a church split that took 220 members and $440,000 tithe out the back door of the church in a single year. We started ministries and closed them, but God's processes also included thousands of people filled with the Holy Ghost, untold miracles of healing, and respect from other ministries that humbles me.

Those experiences were formative foundations that I now understand are the constant process God has chosen for me. Without those foundational formative events, my faith could not have been as great as it is. My prayers and trust in God otherwise might have been underdeveloped.

Recently, I recalled an event from ten years previous. Tracie and I spent a few days in Rockport, Texas, to retreat from some pressures. One day we drove by the church in Aransas Pass, Texas, that my father built when I was about seventeen years old. I pulled into the parking lot and tested the front door to find it unlocked, so I wandered in, walked to the altar area, and wept. At this altar, God confirmed His calling in my life.

Those lonely years when I was the only teenager in the church and served as the de facto assistant pastor came rushing back as I remembered the hundreds of nights I spent alone in that sanctuary. Many times I lay on the altar and wept for the will of God to be done in my life. I laid on the floor by that old altar and soaked in the same anointing God had bestowed upon me when I was young, lonely, confused, and afraid of what God asked me to do. God used that altar for those years in my young life to deepen His formative foundation in me.

The same pulpit was there, and I stood behind it and felt again the surge of first-time anointing. In that place I had first felt the uplift of anointed inspiration. I made a multitude of preaching mistakes behind that desk. I wrecked many good services as a preaching teenager. Dad just kept letting me preach—after all, I was a free preacher—and my dear mom prayed from the second row to the left of the pulpit that God would bless and use me.

One important lesson I learned was transmitted when Mom's prayers began to crescendo while I tried to preach. She would say, "Bless him, Jesus; bless him, Lord!" This was her sweet, maternal way of communicating that my sermon was not going very well. Her prayers were for relief for me, herself, and the rest of the faithful congregation. The louder she prayed, the more I thought she was encouraging me to keep going, so I got louder. When I figured out she was saying, "Hurry up; this is horrible!" I was able to lessen the pain for everyone. And such is what spiritual formation is all about.

One year I was invited home from a camp meeting to preach for an old prophet. He was the kind of prophet who in his day would stop the car, go into the woods, and pray. When he emerged, he would tell those in the car what was going on somewhere. In one such case he came back to the car and told his son that a neighbor had just killed his wife and turned the gun on himself. He added that he was unable to stop the tragedy through intercession. They arrived home, and the police cars were at the neighbors' home. Events had unfolded just as he had shared.

The Saturday night of my visit, the prophet indicated he wanted to go to the little clapboard church in Woden, Texas, to pray for a few minutes. He led me onto the tiny stage and pulled a chair behind the pulpit. He then instructed me to pull my chair between his knees and said, "This is where you are going to pray." He pinned me with his knees, held both of my hands, and began to pray. That interval of prayer to this day is one of my most treasured formative moments. Our prayer that night took me places I had never been, and the new anointing that settled upon me the next morning has never left. God's arrangement of seemingly random events have proven time and time again that His formative process in my life continues.

For five years I sat at the feet of probably the purest prophet the Pentecostal movement has known in the last fifty years. His selfless impartation into me is immeasurable. Lessons he shared, spiritual giftings he placed within me, and prayer meetings, fastings, and times of fellowship remain priceless for me.

When my own ministry began to grow, it seemed my times with him grew fewer and more precious. Dementia began to steal his ability at a much too early age. I watched as he forgot friends and family. The great prophet was disappearing behind a veil of dementia.

However, he never forgot me! He might be lost in the fog of disease, but when he saw me, he would remember. I attribute this to the hundreds of prayer meetings and prophetic impartations we shared.

The day I bumped into him and his wife at a funeral was a bad day for him. He knew no one except me. He held my arm the entire evening until a fellow pastor walked into the room. I watched as the prophet's back straightened. The cloud left his face as he laid hands on the pastor. He spoke clearly a word from God to the man. When he finished, he stepped back, his back slumped, and the cloud returned to his face as again he held my arm.

A few days before he passed away, his family called and said the old prophet's time was close; they would like for me to come. He had not recognized anyone in several days until I walked into the room. He snapped awake, sat up in the bed, and said, "I knew you would come." He prayed over me one last time.

At his funeral I requested the funeral director to allow me to close the casket. I knew it was a strange request but was permitted to do so. While I gently lowered the lid, I laid my hand upon the chest of my now dead prophet. My eyes were the last to look upon him; my hands were the last ones that touched him. His last prayer and prophecy were over me.

As I write this, my emotions rise to the surface. I recall this man and so many others who have participated as instruments of God in His formative process to establish solid foundations in my life. Today, God continues to form His process in my life, and at the same time He uses me to participate in the spiritual formation of the next generation of leaders.

Culture of an Apostolic Pentecostal

The culture of an Apostolic Pentecostal is my lifelong reality—the reality of my childhood upbringing, my worship reality, my consecration reality, and my vocational reality. My earliest memories are of church services, revival meetings, and conferences. I have attended my organization's district camp meeting for fifty-nine consecutive years.

I am an Apostolic Pentecostal. This consciousness brings joy to me, for I have been blessed to live and to work within the vibrant atmosphere of exciting church, incredible worship, dynamic and powerful preaching, and life-changing altar experiences. I have witnessed thousands of miraculous healings. I have seen more prayers answered than I can estimate. There is literally no way to tally the numbers of people with whom I have rejoiced as God filled them with the baptism of the Holy Ghost.

My Pentecostal culture included going to church several times per week. Sunday morning, Sunday night, sometimes a Sunday afternoon service, Monday night prayer meetings, Saturday night prayer meetings, and Wednesday night Bible studies were a way of life. Some Wednesday nights were pretty good, some great, and some not so great.

If the doors were open and the lights were on, we were there. It is still that way for my family. For generations my family has attended every time the doors were open, and we train our next generations that if the doors are open, you better be there! I might have skipped school, skipped curfew, or skipped my homework, but skipping church was non-negotiable. I did not bother to ask, for I knew the answer.

My worship culture reality includes many revivals and special services. Our family spent vacations at conferences and camp meetings. I have never been to Disney World, but I have attended thousands of church meetings!

We prayed! My pastor dad seemed to think that God would hear our prayers better at 5 AM. He would get us out of bed, dress us in jackets over pajamas, and take us to the church to pray. We prayed for our food, our health, the services, our pets, and our money. Literally, the fix-all solution to our lives was simply to pray about it.

I was one of those Pentecostal kids who never had a television in my house. I had a drug problem early on. Dad drug us to prayer. Mom drug us to Sunday school. They both drug us to Wednesday night Bible study, and then they drug us to the altar if they thought we needed it.

Dad pastored one church that needed two thousand dollars per month to pay the church note and light bill. The church was small, so they financed their operations with Pentecostal peanut brittle at one dollar per bag. This computes to two thousand bags of peanut brittle per month, or five hundred bags per week.

On Monday nights, we gathered for the production. The ladies cooked the brittle, the men poured the brittle into aluminum pie pans, we children banged the pie pans on the tables to spread the brittle in the pan uniformly, and the grandmothers bagged the brittle. Somehow, I was always appointed to wash the candy pots.

The next few days we all sold the brittle. Then we had church on Sunday, and Monday night we were back in the kitchen making the next batch of five hundred bags of peanut brittle. I even created my own little jingle while selling my peanut brittle quota.

Hey, diddle diddle,
It's peanut brittle.
You won't get fat if you eat just a little.
You can buy it fast, or you can buy it slow.
And if you like it, brother,
Please buy some mo'.

To this day when I see peanut brittle for sale as I travel, I always check to see if it is Pentecostal peanut brittle. If so, I buy all they have available. I cannot help myself.

Another church Dad pastored sold chicken dinners every Friday to make their church note. Mom and Dad had a system in which they would get up early on Friday, cook the chickens, make the potato salad, and heat up the beans for a couple of hundred chicken dinners. But selling two hundred dinners on Friday meant that somebody must split one hundred chickens in half on Thursday night. This was in the era when chickens were whole and came packed in ice. Early on, my job was the chief chicken splitter. Today, I laugh about it, but those Thursday nights were far from joyful. But, oh, so formative!

Long sermons and long altar services were part of our culture. Sunday night church meant three songs, testimony service (more to come on this subject), special songs (some solo, duet, trio, or whatever other unrehearsed group wanted to share their talent), the offering, an hour-long sermon at least, and then an hour or so in the altar service. Out of those services, though, came thousands of believers who live for God to this day.

Hellfire and brimstone preaching was typical. Preaching that identified sin was acceptable and expected. The preachers had no problem calling out problems and fixing them right there, in the middle of the preaching. The harder the preacher, the better the preacher it seemed. This seems surreal nowadays, but many was the time sinners ran to the altar and repented when the preacher finished his sermon.

Prayer requests were the best, especially when the request and the requester were juicy with local gossip. One lady in a church Dad pastored was married to the town drunk. In one prayer request session, she stood and asked for prayer for her drunkard husband because "he staggered out into the road and got hit by a car, praise the Lord!" But we prayed. The culture of Pentecost was to pray until something happened. The community always knew, if someone had a serious sickness or problem, to get the Pentecostals to pray because they really knew how.

Our culture of Pentecost included embracing holiness. Our ladies wore modest attire. Women dressed like women and men like men. Our ladies wore their hair long, and long meant uncut! Modest faces were good for both the men and the women. Modesty also meant that our men wore longer sleeves and no short pants. I could spend some time here with scriptural validation, but for the purpose of this discussion, our Pentecostal culture was a life of separation from the world. This culture, based in scriptural truth, produced a power that others yearned for.

In those days the Pentecostal culture mandated people not to have television in their homes or to go to the movie theaters, known then as "picture shows." Today's culture of smart phones and computers make that seem out of touch. Those early preachers railed against the evils of Hollywood when the worst thing on TV was *Gilligan's Island*. People mocked our cultural stand, but today when *Sex in the City* can be viewed on one's smart phone, one must appreciate the wisdom of those old-timers.

My Pentecostal culture led me to hundreds of all-night prayer meetings. At watch night services, we prayed out the old year and prayed in the new one. In prayer lines, everybody in the church would walk in a line through the altar area, and the ministry prayed for everybody in the house. Area youth rallies were the highlight of the month. Some areas had "fellowship meetings" where every preacher in the house got to preach for a few minutes. It didn't matter if they could or couldn't preach; they preached!

Does anybody remember those prayer services when the pastor would gather everybody around the front and set a chair in the middle of the group? Anybody who needed "the victory" would sit in the chair, and all the saints would lay hands on and pray for him until he got "the victory"! I may or may not have gotten "the victory" several times without really getting "the victory."

When we had "singings," area churches assembled so anyone who wanted to sing had the chance to do so, whether or not he or she had musical ability. We had some wonderful singers, and we had more than our share of those who appreciated their own singing much more than the rest of us did. But when the anointing settled on a song, heaven responded. Such opportunities were the training grounds for ministers and singers who went on to greater things in the kingdom.

Song services were events to remember. Service may or may not start on time and might or might not start with a chorus. The position of song leader was cherished. The song leader would stand and call for any requests or selections. Unpracticed and unprepared we would launch into singing whatever page number had been requested. The musicians did not need to practice because they could not read music anyway. They all played "by ear." Besides, practicing would interfere with "following the Spirit." To be quite honest, a little more practice might have helped us along the way. But, oh, how the glory would come into those old song services!

Nothing brought more excitement than a good, old-fashioned Pentecostal testimony service! I remember a large lady testifying and swatting at her seven-year-old boy. Unknown to her, she had a garment malfunction, and her skirt was caught up in her enormous . . . well, never mind. You get the picture. Her son was attempting to help her, by gently pulling on the fabric, but she swatted him while testifying. So the little guy deftly reinserted the skirt into the place he was trying to extract it from.

Those old-timers testified of the greatness of God, and many times people would rejoice during the testimony service as other people got saved. One good member would get so excited while testifying that his false teeth would pop out. He would catch them, tuck them in his pocket, and keep right on testifying.

Lingering altar services were a staple of our Pentecostal culture. The pastor would declare the "altars are now open," and people would gather, kneeling and praying for long periods of time. Travailing prayers and intercession would often break out. I remember one Sunday afternoon praying for quite some time for a young man who no longer attended church. I prayed and prayed, asking God to bring that fellow to service "tonight." When he walked into the service and stepped all the way to the altar, I knew I had learned what intercessory prayer was about that day.

The cultural style of Pentecost in those days fit the culture of the moment. It probably would not be well accepted today; however, in a rough-and-tumble blue-collar society, the cultural reality of an old-fashioned Pentecostal service was just what was needed.

Fast forward to our post-Covid, Woke, cancel-culture society with our advanced technology and a culture at war like no other time. The church has no less responsibility to the current culture than did our forefathers when bringing the gospel to their generations.

Advancing technologies and a better educated society have mandated a smoother, more professional presentation of the gospel. Church today is done quite differently than in years past. This generates a nostalgic empty place for the elders who remember the "good old days" and rightfully so.

I was called to do a funeral in a mountainous region of Appalachia during an ice storm. It was quite a challenge just to travel to the service. So I, a Pentecostal preacher, and another more traditional pastor both participated. I listened to that good pastor bemoan the fact that the old songs were ignored for all this "new music." I left that service amused that at least I am not the only pastor caught up in the cultural struggle of church songs in this modern day.

Covid moved many of us to online presentations of our services if we wanted to connect with our members. The challenge of presenting the culture of dynamic Pentecostal services without losing our most incredible giftings to the cameras has been challenging.

Regardless of the culture of church and Pentecost of the late twentieth and early twenty-first centuries, some things absolutely do not change. Methodology is an ever-evolving process; missiology is not. To approach this concept correctly, one must pose a simple question daily: "What is my mission?"

While the Apostolic Pentecostal church has a distinct culture, too many have mistakenly emphasized the methods over the mission. Many of the baby boomer generation placed more emphasis on method than mission. Others have elevated the doctrines of separation over the doctrines of grace, love, Spirit-infilling, and such like.

When one understands that the mission surpasses the method, he has arrived at a place of maturity. On the other hand, methods are not to be disdained, for more times than not, the method has a viable purpose.

Apostolic Pentecostal culture must ever be about mission! This point was impressed on me again to me in the past few weeks. The political and social divide in our country concerning Covid-19 issues has raised the debate of whether the church should take a stand on vaccination issues. I have counseled pastors of late who have lost membership over this issue. Business leaders have reached out for counsel on how they should lead themselves and their businesses with these issues. I began to unravel this process and decision, settled the issue for myself, and then shared this with each leader who sought counsel. It became quite simple to me.

I concluded that I could not confuse my American civil liberties with my God-called mission. While I love my patriotism, I must be more loyal to my mission. Hence, the issue is settled. If being unvaccinated hinders my mission, I will be vaccinated and trust the Lord for His protection and benefits. Mission must remain the priority of the Apostolic Pentecostal culture.

The Apostolic Pentecostal culture has always consisted of these most basic things: powerful prayer, incredible worship, anointed preaching, spiritual demonstration, the operation of spiritual gifts, the working of miracles, life-changing altar experiences, celebratory baptismal services, loyalty to the Bible's example of the New Testament church, and a life of separation from the flesh-gratifying world. These are the non-negotiables of Pentecostal culture. The methods must meet the needs of the current generation.

Just as the children of Issachar had great insight into their spiritual and social cultures, so must the modern-day Issachars seek the understanding of today's cultural challenges. The wisdom needed is not how to adapt the church to the world but rather how the church can invite the world into the culture of Holy Ghost power, deliverance, and demonstration. After all, did not Peter on the Day of Pentecost tell the nations that the promise fulfilled that day was for their generation, the next generation, and even the generations and cultures many miles and years from Jerusalem? Today's culture needs more influence of the Apostolic Pentecostal culture and not less.

Culture of a Pentecostal Preacher

The culture of an Apostolic Pentecostal preacher is my vocational reality. The context and content of my life and livelihood consist of the fact that I am a man of God.

As previously written, I am the product of a multi-generation Pentecostal family. Also, my reality includes my upbringing in the home of a powerful man of God! Dad was called into ministry at the age of eight years when he awoke from a polio-induced coma. His first words upon awaking were: "If Jesus will heal me, then I will preach His gospel for the rest of my life!"

God healed him miraculously in a single service when Dad went to the altar and asked for prayer. Instantly, the brace, with a four-inch platform shoe, around his withered leg got too tight. He took the brace off and saw that his leg had grown four inches immediately!

I grew up literally living with a walking miracle of healing as a testimony of the power of God. For many years that old brace hung on a nail in my grandmother's garage, reminding us of the wonder of the apostolic dimension. Even though God healed Dad and his leg grew four inches, Dad has walked with a limp for seventy-two years. Ironically, with age, his bad leg has become his good leg and his good leg his bad leg. The miracle leg that he has walked on all these years has outlived his leg that did not need healing!

Dad has pastored churches all over Texas and today is retired but still active in the ministry. He has shown by example to all five of his children that God's callings are for a lifetime.

The formation process of God in my life has been multifaceted, and I will share snapshots of those steps that added to my development.

Calling: I was called into the ministry at an early age. Since before my pre-teen years, my calling has been inescapable. I was the kid who toted his Bible to school and taught Bible studies in the library during study hall. The call of God is difficult to explain. One old-timer said, "I cannot explain what the call of God is, but I can tell you what it ain't!" I think I understand him.

Jonah and others showed us the call of God is unshakable and inescapable. When one answers the call, he finds joy in the journey. When one resists that call, God has a way of finding him even if he thinks he are safe while he hides in the bottom of the ocean in the belly of a whale. God told Saul on the highway to Damascus, "Saul, it is hard to kick against the pricks." I too tried kicking against those pointy things God placed around me but to no avail.

My calling led me to Texas Bible College. While I had a vocational scholarship to a secular college, I was led to attend this school rather than seek a secular education. Looking back, I may have benefitted financially by choosing a secular pathway and then answering my call a few years later, but the urgency at that moment said, "Go to Bible school, and find your way into the harvest."

Those years were formative in many aspects as I learned to study, developed the disciplines to be a motivated self-starter, and created relationships with those on the same journey. Building the necessary disciplines for a life in the ministry was quite challenging. Even today I find myself, as an established pastor, constantly honing the skills of my calling, my craft, and my character.

This constant formation has led me back to college at fifty-nine years of age to complete a degree and then at age sixty into graduate school. While in our local church we are in a transitional plan where I am handing the responsibility of the leadership of Conroe Church to the next pastor, I cannot even consider retirement. I was formed, and my lifetime of seeking for greater things from God has placed me on yet another path for greater spiritual formation. Where this journey of graduate school will take me, I am uncertain, but I follow the model of Caleb. I look at the inheritance of a great life yet feel the need to keep stretching and allowing myself to grow and to take in new territory. God's formation of me is yet in process, and I echo great-great-great-grandpa Caleb, "Give me this mountain!"

Craft: Ministry requires unique skills or craft. Certain skills must be developed. Many of the skills required for the ministry are seen on Sunday such as dress, delivery, poise, anointing, and content. However, the unseen things are more important. One must constantly plan, prepare, ponder, meditate, and pray. One must develop sensitivity for the moment and listen for the voice of God. Such things cannot be taught in a classroom but must come by constantly walking in the presence of the Lord. If one ignores craft and depends upon calling alone, he will fail. At the same time, the development and perfecting of the craft of ministry when there is no calling will result in frustration when doors do not open.

Character: Calling and craft alone can never sustain a ministry. Character is the third leg to the stool of ministry.

The character the minister exhibits defines his ministry more than his calling or his crafting. Far too many ministers have been called and pursued the development of ministerial craft while failing to understand the most important leg on the ministerial stool is character.

The greatest biblical example of this is probably Samson. Called before his birth, he had developed strength and craft to be a very fierce deliverer for the people of God. However, the weakness of his character caused his eventual fall. While we celebrate the final victory of Samson, his life no doubt is better described as a spiritual tragedy. Too many skilled and God-called men have overlooked the importance of their own integrity.

King David had found success and decided to stay home from the war when he succumbed to the temptation of Bathsheba. This would evolve into a conspiracy to cover his sin with the murder of her husband. While God could and did forgive David's sin, his lack of integrity marked his life negatively and brought painful consequences for years.

I have witnessed too many called and developed ministries come to naught simply because of the character issues of the minister. In other cases, it seems that a minister's lack of integrity seems to be ignored and even promoted. Time is the best proving ground for these issues. One must never forget that our Lord said that everything done in secret will be revealed.

Simply put, every God-called minister must spend as much time developing his personal character as he does building his personal ministry. When you see that three-legged stool of the ministry topple, examine what happened, and you will find the only broken leg likely will be the character leg of the ministry. Character can survive without great craft skills, but a calling and developed craft are not sustainable without a character of integrity.

Considering this, I am assured the culture of an Apostolic Pentecostal minister (and this should hold true with any minister) demands integrity. The ministry is a place of trust. People trust you into their lives. They trust their children to your leadership. When seeking counsel or guidance, good people open their hearts and share intimate details with the understanding they can and should trust their minister. Churches trust their pastors to conduct business matters on behalf of the church. The pastor is a representative of the church to the local community. Such trust mandates the minister conduct himself as worthy of said trust. He cannot do so if he has integrity issues.

I once heard an example of a pastor who needed to correct the behavior of a young teenager in the youth group. The young person got upset at the pastoral correction and blurted in typical teenager fashion, "You don't have any right to tell me what to do because I know you have been talking to my momma on the phone late at night!"

When there is a breach in the wall of integrity, all trust is eroded. Once a minister surrenders his moral authority, he is powerless in some situations.

The culture of an Apostolic preacher provides many blessings to the minster. He oftentimes is well traveled. His family enjoys the benefits of those travels. They have many friends and relationships due to this exposure to other ministers and their families. His family often is invited to nice restaurants or the homes of church families. At the same time, the minister's family is like any other family and needs to be reminded to appreciate their blessings. Often, when our children were still at home, I would pause a nice meal in a restaurant and remind the family we were the beneficiaries of the generosity of good church folks' faithful stewardship.

Our kids came home from a youth event and were playing a game called "Name That Saint." Apparently, the young people had enjoyed a time of imitating church members while others tried to name the church member mimicked. It was a cute, harmless exercise in human behavior, but as a father and pastor it became important to teach my children that the innocence of a fun game should never be allowed to hinder their view and appreciation of the good people entrusted to our family's care.

Part of the culture of a minister is that he lives in a glass house. His family lives in that same house. Frequently, the minister and his family face unrealistic criticism from those they lead. While this is easily accepted by the minister, his children are not so well equipped to handle such things. Too often the children of a pastor have unjustly felt the sharp criticisms from church members who really had an issue with their preacher dad but chose to point their criticism toward the preacher's kid to deflect their own shortcomings. Far too many preachers' kids have drifted from the church simply because unrealistic expectations of church members upon them and their parents have created deep resentment in their own hearts.

On the other hand, many children of ministers have successfully navigated those times of criticism and felt their own call into the ministry. These young people are often considered to have been handed a gospel "silver spoon" and are accused of benefiting from the nepotistic efforts of their fathers'. While this may be the truth in some cases, a young person reared in the home of pastor indeed has a head start on other aspiring young ministers due to the simple fact he/she understands the culture of the ministry, having grown up in it. Regardless of whether one was raised in a minister's home or not, the reality is that one must learn to live in an environment of transparency that comes with residing in that glass house that often comes without curtains.

Conferences, camp meetings, and other fellowship-type of gatherings of ministers are vital to the spiritual health of a minister and his family. While from the outside such meetings look like just more church, there is strength when men and women of God gather for worship and renewal. Relationships are formed and maintained during these times. Ministers gain emotional and spiritual strength when they are with other ministers. The culture of an Apostolic Pentecostal preacher cannot survive without these gatherings. In many cases it takes all the finance and strength the minister can gather just to make the trip, but when he leaves the meeting to travel back to his calling, he does so with great faith and fire in his spirit.

The culture of an Apostolic Pentecostal preacher must face the politics of the church. It has been my experience that when you have two people involved in any project, one is going to rise to the leadership position. Such relationships require human government. Human government's greatest weakness is the politics of those humans involved. Such human arrangements evolve into many discussions around dinner tables, phone calls, and even in modern-day internet forums and friend groups. These heated discussions are no different from ministerial debates we read of in the Book of

Acts. These discussions are hot, fiery, emotional, and, oh, so formative! The words of elder ministers as younger ministers listen to the wisdom of bygone years are life-giving.

I can remember sitting around tables in awe of the discussions of the elders. Now I have become one of those elders, and I trust that I can impart as much to the next generation of leaders as was imparted unto me.

The minister must be careful never to allow the differences between brethren to become something that brings a break in fellowship or relationship. Too often good men have allowed an issue to divide them from the fellowship of their brothers, and when isolated, that good man opens an inroad for the enemy. My fellow minister, never let anything separate you from the fellowship of the body. Human government and politics are not worth losing the fellowship of your brother. Do not let a simple human disagreement undo years of what God has formed in your life and ministry.

The ministerial body of the Apostolic Pentecostal movement is a brotherhood that I call the "thin black line." We the fellowship of ministers are part of that line. I too often attend meetings, notice gaps in that line, and realize another man is missing. We need each other.

This became very clear to me years ago when my fifteen-month-old granddaughter drowned in front of our house. Suddenly, that precious little life was gone. I was lost in grief. Tracie was overcome in brokenness. We did our best to be there for our kids, who had lost their baby, but we were as broken as they.

At the viewing of her little body, our church, our city, and our ministerial brotherhood came to support us. The police volunteers who were parking cars and moving the line stopped counting after three thousand people had come to pay their respects. More than fifteen hundred attended the funeral. We will never know the actual number of attendees, but we will never forget the brotherhood who showed up when we needed it.

This depicts the culture of the Apostolic Pentecostal ministry better than any illustration I can share. As I write this paragraph, I received word of a minister's wife who passed minutes ago. I attended her husband's funeral fifteen years ago. I have been a mentor to her children, and now she has passed. I will be attendance at her funeral in the next few days because that is what the culture of an Apostolic Pentecostal preacher prescribes.

During the Revolutionary War, British pamphleteers derided what became known as the Black Robed Regiment. A ministerial coalition led by Pastor John Muhlenberg proclaimed the need for freedom of religion should be preached loud and fiery. Then he and other pastors would lead volunteer regiments into battle. It is said that long before the military maneuvers began, the spiritual maneuvers were in progress in the pulpits of the burgeoning republic.

Recently reading of this historical marvel, I reflect upon a reality I find in today's ministerial climate. The ministerial body of the Apostolic Pentecostal movement is akin to a brotherhood. This Thin Black Line or men of the cloth wear black suits on Sundays and at weddings, funerals, and conferences. They stand to declare the gospel of the New Birth message. As years pass, I see holes form in that line where another good Black Line warrior has exited the battle through natural progression as age or death or, more tragically, through fatigue or defeat.

Such stresses include the pressure of people, pressure of the world, pressure to compromise, pressure to give up, and the pressure of family. With the stress of budgets come boards who have unrealistic expectations. These pastor-warriors battle things that are not of flesh and blood but war against spirits of darkness, highly positioned wickedness, and even demonic dominions whose assignment is to wear out and paralyze the man of God.

To work alongside these warriors is a singular honor. These men are warriors and brothers in combat, and this brotherhood understood post-traumatic stress disorder long before the term became common. Too often I have grieved the loss of the ministry of a great kingdom warrior for the simple reason he is suffering from PTSD. Such stressful situations indeed are a confirmed part of a minister's formative process. Still, I grieve.

While this paragraph may wander from the purpose of this book, I have personally pledged to stand alongside any minister who is weary in the battle and to help lift his hands to God as did Aaron and Hur for Moses.

The culture of an Apostolic Pentecostal minister is one of sacrifice and pain. Oh, we look good on Sunday. We dress in our good suit and have our white shirt pressed sharply and tie done just right. We are manicured and coiffured so the cameras will get our good side no matter which way we are looking. In reality, there is much pain. People disappoint us often. Betrayal is a human weakness, and much humanity is found within the church. Sin makes its way into the best of families.

I will never forget the first time I felt the pains of betrayal from a wonderful family I trusted implicitly. I had retreated into myself and began to ask God why when He spoke clearly through His Word to me. "I asked some disciples if they were going to leave Me too."

With this revelation I realized that God had felt every human emotion of disappointment I was feeling. As this understanding came to me, my wife stepped into the church office with a little present for me that holds a place in my office thirty years later. To really know Jesus, one will know Him in the fellowship of His suffering as well as the fellowship of His miraculous power.

A further word on the pain of suffering for the ministry: When I feel new pain, I have learned to be patient. God is leading me through this new pain because I will be leading others through something similar very soon. It is astounding to realize God forms me so I can form someone else.

It seems that spiritual formation is never complete. I find that as soon as I think I am graduating, along comes the next lesson.

Paul wrote that he was all things to all men, and it was interpreted to the proverbial Pentecostal preacher's handbook that the Pentecostal preacher must be all things to all men. We find ourselves being lawyer, counselor, and plumber to the church membership. Somehow it was put upon us that we had to have all the answers. Newsflash, we do not! While seeking pastoral advice is a very good thing, pastors must recognize they need not be the Messiah.

Many years ago during an annual leadership planning meeting, I grew frustrated because it seemed the whole session slowed down while we all figured out how many cans of beans would be needed for a dinner. The leader found it important that the pastor (me) tell them how many beans to buy. I waxed eloquent on the fact that I did not care how many beans they bought, and it was time they grew up and learned to read the number of servings on the can and multiply that by the number of people they wanted to have beans. Grow up! I seem to remember explaining that the first deacons were appointed to feed the widow women so the preachers could focus on the Sunday sermon. Everybody laughed, and we went on.

The next year at the planning meeting I opened with prayer, and when I opened my eyes every leader had a can of green beans sitting on the table in front of him and a big cheesy grin on his face. Twenty-five years later, I have not counted a single bean!

Honor is often extended to the ministry. Churches love to share their appreciation to their pastors. These moments are always awkward but important in the development of a healthy church.

Long before October was known for clergy appreciation, I wanted to teach Conroe Church to honor the ministry without telling them to buy me gifts. God allowed a wonderful, retired minister to be with us for a few years. I felt led to begin to honor him publicly to teach our young church plant that honoring the ministry was important. The dear minister and his wife were awkward and reluctant to receive such accolades and honors.

I would have them sing a song on Sunday before the camp meeting and then tell the people that sounded like a five-dollar song, and I needed a bunch of five-dollar bills on the altar for these elders. We would collect several hundred dollars, put all that cash in the elder's pocket, and tell him to have a good time at the camp meeting.

He called me to his house one day and told me I had to stop honoring them. I replied, "Elder, I need you to help me to teach these young converts that honoring the ministry is important, and the only way I know to teach them is to show them. So I need you to stop making a fuss and enjoy the blessings!"

Today, Conroe Church honors us more than they should. Several years ago, I had to form a committee to handle all the pastoral honoring they were doing because literally it was every month and too much.

I have chosen to include this to contrast the difference between our young church of thirty years ago and the mature Conroe Church today. Early on I had to train these people that it was important to honor the ministry. As time has gone on, their honor became too much. The integrity formed in me over the years insisted that I teach them that honoring the ministry is important, but creating an extravagant, flamboyant entitlement culture is not right either.

The culture of Pentecostal ministry must continue to be a life of servant leadership. Selfless sacrifice is simply part of the culture of ministry.

The culture of a Pentecostal preacher/pastor must nurture the baby to maturity and then let that saint of God grow to become a leader on his own gifts. Train, grow, release, and then train more. Then the training pastor can train a trainer, the pastor trains the trainer, and eventually the pastor seldom gets his hands involved in the menial tasks of the church.

Spiritual formation is never a quick process and can be many years or even a lifetime in the making. My formation began long before I was welcomed into this world in

1961. Yesterday, my wife said she needed to share a sermon with me and began to talk about Zacchaeus. Her flash of revelatory inspiration may well have come from some social media post, but she was excited to inform me that long before Zacchaeus needed to climb that tree, God knew that moment was coming. The tree had to be planted and allowed to grow to the place of maturity so it could support the weight of a man desperate for a glimpse of Jesus.

God's process in my life has been just as real. We planted Conroe Church in 1990. I came to Conroe and rented a house for my family, and the first time Tracie saw the house was when we backed the U-Haul up the driveway. Little did I know that God had His hand on that address seventy-five years before.

One day the doorbell rang, and a couple stood with that most fearful introduction, "We are from the government." It turns out they were representatives for the Environmental Protection Agency, and they were evacuating the neighborhood for the next nine months. We learned they wanted to visit with us concerning our options for temporary housing and reimbursement. We were first-year church planters. In those years church planters did not have the benefit of start teams and start budgets. Needless to say, we were financially embarrassed. Financially embarrassed in the Greek is simply "broke!"

Our visitors began to explain that the EPA was arranging for our temporary housing and living expenses for the next several months. Long story short, the EPA would pay us about five thousand dollars per month not to live in our house. God's process and provision had set up this circumstance for our benefit.

We came to learn that seventy-five years ago the site where our house sat had been a creosote plant. Railroad ties and telephone poles were pressure treated with creosote there. The EPA had deemed the entire neighborhood toxic, and the land not covered in pavement had to be abated. As I see it, in about 1920 when men made telephone poles in our neighborhood, angels allowed extra creosote to splash on the ground because God knew He had a young preacher coming to plant a church. That minister would need five thousand dollars per month for his first year in Conroe.

God's process began long before God had called me, sent me to Bible college, and allowed Tracie and me to wed. God permitted all these and many other events to prepare Tracie and me to survive that first year as church planters.

The New Birth Culture

The New Birth culture was established in the early church on the Day of Pentecost. The church grew exponentially. Then the persecution of believers was set in motion by the Roman government. Instead of quenching the spread of this new spiritual phenomenon, the heavy boots of persecution scattered the embers of the Pentecostal experience. What began on the Day of Pentecost in Jerusalem spread to the ends of the known world.

Luke in Acts recorded the spiritual display of fire above each of those in the upper room. We learn that these uneducated men from the area of Galilee spoke in a variety of languages understood by the pilgrims visiting Jerusalem for the Pentecost holiday. On that birthday of the church, Peter stood and preached, offering an explanation to the observers that they were witnessing the fulfillment of the words of the ancient prophet Joel, who had foretold of a Spirit outpouring. Following Peter's explanation, three thousand souls received the new birth experience we know as the gift of the Holy Ghost. The apostle Peter introduced a new doctrine that day that continues yet today.

What happened in Jerusalem that day was the advent of the New Birth culture in which I was formed. I grew up watching as many experienced their personal Pentecost. I received my own Pentecostal experience on February 14, 1969. God filled me with the Holy Ghost that day. I was a Pentecostal before being Pentecostal was cool!

The new birth is demonstrated in Acts 2 and defined in a single verse (38). Peter answered the questions of the pilgrims by saying that they should repent, be baptized in the name of Jesus for the remission of their sins, and be filled with the gift of the Holy Ghost. He continued with the admonition that this experience was for each of them, their next generations, and anyone at a great distance, whether generational, geographical, or cultural.

This without debate is the simple new birth that the early church; the students in Topeka, Kansas; those at Azusa Street; and millions of others have received. This experience is not respective of persons, race, creed, or social status. Both the educated and the pauper stand side by side in the presence of the Almighty and experience the same power of being born again.

I lead a small group monthly in my home. Represented in this group are a counselor, a certified public accountant, a medical doctor, an assistant district attorney, a business owner, a medical assistant, a recent college graduate, a college freshman, a fourth-year college student, a security guard, a disabled man who has a failed kidney transplant and a prosthetic eye, a three-time heart transplant recipient with a kidney transplant as well, a registered nurse, a doctoral candidate who is researching a cure for the cancer that took his mother, a stay-at-home dad, a corporate vice-president, a pastor's wife, and myself. I marvel every month when this group gathers, for they represent the spectrum of success and struggle. Yet the commonality bringing unity to the group is the new birth. Great experiences create movements, and movements create culture. Such happens in and through everyone with the new birth as in the Book of Acts.

Saul of Tarsus was the cursing and killing machine of early Christians until his Damascene Freeway experience, after which he became the chief proponent of this gospel. Contrast the early Saul to the apostle Paul when he wrote to Philemon, insisting his runaway slave, Onesimus, might be a natural slave, but he was also a brother in Christ.

During the early 1900s the New Birth message spread from Topeka to Houston, west to Los Angeles, and then swept back across North America, transforming every life it touched. It removed racial barriers and transcended social and economic prejudice. Young and old alike can worship together because movements create culture!

This emerging culture manifested in tent meetings, brush arbors, storefronts, and street corners. With time it moved into clapboard buildings and then began to take on nicer and more impressive addresses. It did not matter if the meeting was held in a storefront or a cathedral; the movement produced a culture of exciting fellowship.

People pray aloud. Boisterous worship can be expected. Preachers exude faith and anointing. Altars produce new spiritual children. Healings are common. Baptisms are celebrated. Even in this technologically advanced day when services are freely streamed, the culture of the new birth cannot be equaled in depth or power.

For many years the established church resisted and mocked what unfolded in this cultural tidal wave. Today, even the most liturgical of religious groups will allow the lifting of hands. Multiple services are offered with various worship styles accepted. Houston, Texas, has a Catholic Charismatic church that embraces speaking in tongues. The New Birth culture influences the most unlikely of churches.

Just outside my city is a small city known as Cut and Shoot, Texas. One hundred years ago, the New Birth culture crept into the community. There were many saloons in the area. A preacher filled with the Holy Ghost came to the area and began holding services in the community center, and the New Birth culture began to transform the area. The saloon owners began to see a reduction in their liquor sales because their regular customers were switching fellowship circles and cultures. The saloon owners banded together and got the church kicked out of the community center. The preacher without a fuss set up a tent and continued bringing a new culture to the people.

The saloon owners paid a group of rowdy men to go to the tent to cause trouble. That night the rowdies threw tomatoes into the tent, shot out the oil-burning lamps, and cut the tent ropes. But the revival fires were not quenched. The area became known as Cut and Shoot because the Pentecostal tent was cut down and shot up that night. After more than one hundred years, the culture shift of that revival continues. Great moments create their own culture.

There is no preaching like that of a God-called, Holy Ghost-filled, praying preacher. Regardless of the education or age of the preacher, the anointing breaks the yoke of spiritual bondage. I have seen orators move the hearts of God's people. Likewise, I marvel when a young Bible-school student is used of God, having equal effect.

We had a Bible-school preacher with a seizure disorder speak to our church plant on our first Easter evening service. We had been here for only three months and had about twenty in attendance that evening. Seven people in the service had never received the gift of the Holy Ghost. After the young preacher boy finished his very bad sermon in a very few minutes, he asked if anybody wanted the Holy Ghost. In the next fifteen minutes, all seven were filled with the Spirit! That service began a culture of new babies in Conroe Church that continues thirty years later.

The New Birth culture is filled with people of prayer. Prayer warriors understood travailing and intercessory prayer long before the neo-Pentecostal preachers began preaching about spiritual warfare. It was common for the preacher or elders to show up where someone was sick and begin to pray. They would pray until something happened. Today, Pentecostal websites and prayer hotlines are filled with the requests of those in need, for they understand that the Pentecostals know how to touch God.

The New Birth culture produced waves of evangelism. In early years, teams of young people traveled and witnessed. Churches learned to hold street meetings and knock doors. Every church had a bus ministry. Today, those forms of evangelism have morphed into social media outreach efforts, services are broadcast, and podcasts strategically reach out. Regardless of the method of evangelism, where you find the New Birth culture, you will find some form of evangelism alive and well.

The traditional Pentecostal people are known for their manner of dress. The culture of the new birth produced an entire genre of hair and fashion styles. The ladies wear modest dresses, their hair long, and very little cosmetics. The men lead their families in modesty. While many have been critical of the modest dress styles, one cannot deny that a distinct difference in the atmosphere of worship prevails when modesty is practiced.

The New Birth culture is a culture of generosity. I find it amazing when a spirit of giving comes into a service, and the greatest financial miracles seem to happen in the most unlikely of congregations. Our people are tithers and have learned the power of God's provision when they submit to God's financial plan for their lives.

Oh, the excitement the New Birth culture has produced in a baptismal service! In the early days when the churches had no baptismal tanks, the saints gathered at a creek, river, beach, or bayou and baptized by torch light or car headlights. People would be buried in baptism in the name of Jesus, and the saints rejoiced. Many repentant baptismal candidates received the gift of the Holy Ghost while still in the water.

As churches prospered, the baptismal tanks improved. Seldom do you see an unheated tank. Some churches hold baptismal Sundays when scores of people are baptized in pools of water brought in for the big day. The atmosphere surrounding the baptism will be filled with exuberant rejoicing and worship. The music will be loud, and the saints will be celebrating in praise.

Pentecostal worship services were exciting long before the modern worship industry began. Previously, there might be an old piano or guitar. During the mid-1900s, the Hammond organ made its way to the Pentecostal church. Song leaders gave way to worship leaders and teams of singers. With the advance of technology, synthesized instruments replaced the old upright pianos. The grand pianos utilized for years were replaced with keyboards. Notwithstanding the changing styles of the music, the anointing and exuberance have never changed. Old songbooks have grown dusty because the songbook can hold only two or three hundred songs. Today thousands of songs are projected onto screens, and people still rejoice. I find it amazing that the New Birth culture brought a worship style that even denominational churches are duplicating.

In conversation with a mentor recently, we discussed this New Birth culture, and he shared the following. The New Birth can be viewed through three distinct lenses.

1. *Doctrinal lens:* There is a distinct doctrinal approach with the new birth, scriptural context I have not endeavored to prove in this writing. I have simply shared as common acceptance the doctrines Peter gave us on the Day of Pentecost.
2. *Practical lens:* Spirit living is really a quite practical lifestyle.
3. *Experiential lens:* The Pentecostal experience is like no other. This experience created what I have referred to as the New Birth culture.

Doctrinal and practical applications are wonderful, but what brings the New Birth culture home to the heart and life of every believer is the experience. The old chorus we used to sing said, "Something got ahold of me. I went there to fight, but—oh, my!—that night God's power got ahold of me!" What an experience!

The new birth produced a movement that resulted in a distinct culture. My formative process is simple in that I was born into this culture rather than having to discover it after a search through other avenues. I have chosen to remain, and I have devoted my life to the biblical doctrines found within that culture. Through and through I affirm my loyalty to the same gospel introduced to the world on the Day of Pentecost. I was Pentecostal long before Pentecostal was cool!

Formation of a Christian

Defining moments seldom appear as such at first glance. In retrospect, a moment emerges clearly as not just another but *the* moment! Pivotal moments come cloaked in routine, regularity, and even mundaneness. Then appears the genesis of great achievements in one's life. The moment appears to be normal and is anything but normal, for the decisions made in that instant change one's trajectory.

Lance Armstrong, the former road-racing cyclist, won the Tour de France for seven consecutive years from 1999 to 2005. To the world his career and ability seemed unequaled until he confessed to using performance-enhancing drugs and was stripped of his racing titles. No doubt he encountered many defining moments in his pursuit to be the best in his sport. However, it is safe to assume his most defining moment happened when he accepted his first performance enhancer. His prior great moments dissolved in a single decision. The champion Armstrong is now known as a doper.

Not all moments are created equal. It was my forty-ninth birthday. Tracie and I had taken a few days off to relax in Hot Springs, Arkansas. We sat lakeside, enjoying a nice breakfast and time together, when I became pensive. I considered my life to date and could find little to criticize. I thought of the reality of my aging process; in just 365 days I would enter my fifth decade. I was turning fifty! Tracie and I talked again of realized and unrealized dreams while these thoughts ran in my mind.

I interrupted Tracie's conversation. "Next year on my fiftieth birthday, I am giving myself a gift of fifty pounds!" This was quite random. Tracie grew quiet. I continued, "For too long I have allowed my weight to take care of itself, and it is time I take control of me. So I am giving myself a fifty-pound birthday present next year."

When I returned home, I joined the YMCA and created a new relationship with the elliptical machine. I hated that guy. The first day I could do less than a minute, but I persisted. By month's end, I could stay on the machine thirty minutes. My daily routine shifted. I left the house every morning by 5:30 and spent time on the elliptical machine. My endurance time, resistance, and incline increased. My breathing began to improve. I spent thirty minutes per day on the machine, then forty-five, and then daily sixty minutes on that demon machine. My weight began to change. I had to buy new clothing. I liked the new me!

On my fiftieth birthday, I planned my personal party. My day started at 5:30 with two bottles of water and a candy bar, just in case. I climbed on my elliptical friend and started my party. Two hours and two minutes later I stopped the machine, but my party continued. I still had a bottle of water and the candy bar unopened. My breathing was steady, my heart rate about 130 bpm. I moved my party to the scale to open my birthday present to myself of eighty-eight pounds lost! By myself I celebrated. I sang, "Happy birthday to me." After all, it was my party. It was my gift to me!

Discipline is a gift one gives himself. I often tell young people that they alone determine the quality of life they desire. They must get themselves out of bed every day. They must be on time to school or work. They must groom themselves. Their schoolwork is their responsibility. The same is true for each of us. More than once, I have taken my sock drawer to a meeting with young people and explained that nobody but them can bring order to their most intimate places of life. Everybody must match and fold his or her own socks. The only true form of discipline is self-discipline.

To this point I have shared my understanding of spiritual formation and the processes God has chosen for me. I have celebrated God's activity in my formative process. I attempted to describe great spiritual transformations and the distinct experience of my vocational and worship context. I have displayed victories and even times of brokenness with you. I introduced you to my family and Conroe Church. I talked about myself much more than I am comfortable with. This project is my assessment of God's formation in my life. This is my looking at me and inviting you into the conversation. Thank you for sharing this time with me.

Now I share my part of the formative process. The spiritual disciplines are a mandate. There are no shortcuts in the formative process. God forms us, but much of His formation is painful and demands our willing cooperation and self-denial. God's redemption, grace, mercy, and forgiveness are free, but they will cost you everything.

Jesus shared a most astounding challenge with His disciples immediately after calling Peter "Satan." In one verse Peter was handed the keys to the kingdom of heaven, and in the next Jesus compared him to Satan. Growing is not easy. Our Lord endeavored to "fast grow" His chosen men for their mission. *Then said Jesus unto his disciples, If any man will come after me, let him deny himself, and take up his cross, and follow me* (Matthew 16:24).

Jesus offered them kingdom success in a single sentence of self-denial, cross bearing, and following the Master. Nothing has changed. It never will. The spiritual disciplines are gifts only the believer can give himself.

A Journey into Disciplines

My professor posed the unwelcome question: "How are you with the disciplines?"

I decided to answer the question with a question, in a supposed imitation of Jesus. "What is your description of the disciplines?"

"Oh, you know, prayer, fasting, study, worship, and giving," he replied.

To his probing I countered—or evaded—with a nonchalant answer, "Oh, I have been teaching them for nearly forty years of ministry." I was pretty sure I had offered a great reply.

His rejoinder: "I am sending you something."

My email dinged, and I opened a link to Richard J. Foster's *Celebration of Discipline: The Path to Spiritual Growth*. This book and a couple of others like it became my new old friends.

Foster took me on a journey of meditation, prayer, fasting, study, simplicity, solitude, submission, service, confession, worship, guidance, and celebration. I found the book difficult to digest the first time through. I read it again two days later and began to understand. On the third reading, I grasped and admired the spirit of this classic masterpiece.

Robin Johnston's *Spiritual Disciplines* added much to my growing awareness of disciplines that have all found their unique niche in my journey of spiritual pursuits. By mistake I purchased *Spiritual Disciplines for the Christian*

Life by Donald S. Whitney and increased my armory of works on spiritual discipline.

Immediately I recognized four discomfiting realities. I framed them into brutally honest statements.

1. I may have been teaching the disciplines for many years, but I was no expert.
2. I need to be an expert.
3. I want to be an expert in them!
4. I will never possess these disciplines until they possess me.

> *And every man that striveth for the mastery is temperate in all things. Now they do it to obtain a corruptible crown; but we an incorruptible* (1 Corinthians 9:25).

As a graduate student striving for a master of arts degree in Christian leadership, I reach for mastery only to find I am still in spiritual preschool. Like Paul affirmed concerning himself, spiritual awakening rumbles deep in me. *Not as though I had already attained, either were already perfect: but I follow after, if that I may apprehend that for which also I am apprehended of Christ Jesus* (Philippians 3:12).

I found myself trying to apprehend what had apprehended me! God had been doing His part in my spiritual formation journey. However, this journey cannot be a simple one-way apprehension. God has always done His part, but my lack of self-awareness in these disciplines evidenced my failure to pursue God as hard as He had pursued me. God had apprehended me. I must apprehend Him!

Hence, the spiritual disciplines became a fresh priority as I partnered with the apostle Paul.

> *[For my determined purpose is] that I may know Him [that I may progressively become more deeply and intimately acquainted with Him, perceiving and recognizing and understanding the wonders of His Person more strongly and more clearly], and that I may in that same way come to know the power outflowing from His resurrection [which it exerts over believers], and that I may so share His sufferings as to be continually transformed [in spirit into His likeness even] to His death, [in the hope]* (Philippians 3:10, *Amplified Bible*).

I uncovered and compiled valuable insights during my study of Richard J. Foster's *Celebration of Discipline* and Robin Johnston's *Spiritual Disciplines*, and I present them in the following pages for your edification as well.

The Discipline of Meditation

Meditation consists of simply listening to God's voice and then obeying His words. There is no great mystery to meditation, nor is there a literal meditative position one must arrange himself into. Rather, meditation is the simple, quiet attitude of listening for God.

Adam had this great privilege in the Garden of Eden, but the clamor of Eve and the serpent distracted him from the still, small, daily voice. Moses interacted with God when He separated himself from the camp of Israel and came face to face with his Friend.

Meditation requires that we create a time and place to commune quietly with the Master. Communing with Him is the mere silence of adoring attention to Him and the reverent acceptance of His whispers. The old prophet was distracted with the noise of thunder and wind, but after the noise subsided, he could hear the still, small voice of our Lord.

Meditation is not necessarily prayer. Prayer might include meditation, but most meditation takes place in a still place. Prayer may demand strenuous intercession, the clamor of travail, or joyful thanks for the great things a great God has done. But meditation is quiet, contemplative communion with the heart and mind of God.

Imagine the communion when Adam walked daily with God! He participated in naked and vulnerable daily conversations with the Creator. Adam knew the safety of trusting his vulnerabilities to his Maker. Is it any wonder that, when he chose in a single moment to trust the whispers from the serpent over his meditative communion with the Creator, he felt stripped, naked, and dirty? Literally, he tried to cover his sinfulness with leaves when he heard the daily invitation from the Lord, "Adam?"

Somewhere along my path of vocational ministry, I discovered my personal meditations were more than sacred. I might be driving down the highway, and in the silence of the car my mind and spirit sought the face of God. While preparing for a funeral or wedding, I would tell my wife, "I must get somewhere for a few moments just to be still." In that stillness I can hear Him. After such moments seldom do I depend upon prepared notes for the wedding or funeral, for I have heard His whispers. Jesus' words for the moment of comfort become a wellspring from the Master rather than rich prose from the pastor.

Sunday mornings are my personal time. As a matter of fact, I was prepared to write this section last evening, but I wanted to write of my meditations during the most sacred meditative appointment of my week. Early Sunday mornings are my alone time with Jesus.

On Sunday morning I arise early. Long before the sun appears, I prepare for the day. Most Sundays before 6 AM I have showered, dressed, donned my tie—the tie is important to me, for I want God to know I am ready for my time with Him—and made my way to my office at Conroe Church. This is my routine whether I am speaking that day or not. If I am traveling, my schedule is the same. I dress and will be in a corner of the hotel lobby because I have a planned, interactive session with the Lord. How many white-shirt-clad, tie-wearing meditants does one see in a hotel breakfast area on a Sunday morning before 6 AM? This is my time to visit with the Lord.

Long ago, Conroe Church opted to respect my parking place and put my name on a "reserved" sign. I removed the sign, but they still respect my place, probably because my vehicle arrives every Sunday long before the sun comes up and I park before most of the church has awakened. This is my time; this is God's time. Even this morning I listened carefully for Him. Sometimes He says nothing, for I am comfortable not only with His still, small voice but also with His silence. I have missed some of our appointments, but He has never missed one!

I have a special place at the altar of Conroe Church as well. Several years ago, while taking down Easter program décor, someone made a small gash in the carpet of our altar steps. The damage was too minor to repair and was ignored. One day in a season of brokenness and prayer, I was praying and then meditating with my face in the carpet. As I listened for God to remember me, I opened my eyes, and that small gashed spot in the carpet was before my eyes. In an instant, that "spot" became "my spot," and never a week goes by when I do not spend some time there. I know this is juvenile for some, but I have regularly met with my Master in that place. He has whispered to me there. He has been silent with me there. "My spot" is a place of reflective interactive communion and meditation with Him!

At times I yearn for "my spot." "My spot" is not intrinsically holy; rather, I liken it to Moses' holy ground. I am safe at "my spot." I am vulnerable in "my spot." God speaks to me there. I slow down and get still enough to hear His still, small voice amid the clamor of my own schedule.

Meditating and listening for the voice of God are essential for the spiritual formation of my life. His miraculous power might be whispered in my ear today; however, if I do not separate myself from the bustle of modern life and retreat to a quiet place, I might just miss the moment of His heavenly voice.

The Discipline of Prayer

Prayer changes things. While meditation is silent yearning that listens for the voice of God, prayer is verbal communication with the Lord that should be constant and clear. Perpetual, heartfelt, and often should our prayers be. *Pray without ceasing* (1 Thessalonians 5:17).

Prayer brings transformation and change. The more we pray, the more God-like we become. The one who prays more desires more prayer. King David's desire for more spiritual matters prompted him to forsake the creature comforts of his king-sized bed long before kings were expected to arise to attend to kingly matters. The earthly king sought the heavenly King. *Early will I seek thee* (Psalm 63:1).

The early church leaders were burdened with the care of the widows and thus unable to focus on their more spiritual responsibilities. As a result, they appointed deacons or servant leaders to attend to the menial duties so the apostles could focus on prayer and the Word.

When Jonah found himself at the bottom of the sea, he prayed from the belly of the whale. In the darkest part of their night while incarcerated and shackled, "Paul and Silas prayed, and sang praises unto God."

The upper room was filled with the prayers of faithful people on the Day of Pentecost. By some reckonings, the crowd began with about 500 souls and dwindled to 120. However, the prayer meeting continued, and in an instant, God filled them all with the Holy Ghost.

71

Paul preached long into the evening, and Eutychus fell asleep and out the window, breaking his neck. But the apostle Paul prayed, and the young man was the featured guest at the fellowship dinner following the service.

Jesus shared what we call the Lord's Prayer with the initial words, "When ye pray"! He granted the assumption that they would pray and that their prayers were inevitable and expected. We celebrate and recite the Lord's Prayer often but hastily pass over the commanding assumption the Lord has for us in Luke 11:2, "When ye pray." Matthew's account of the lesson indicated the Lord's clear instructions concerning how they should pray.

> *Our Father which art in heaven, Hallowed be thy name. Thy kingdom come. Thy will be done in earth, as it is in heaven. Give us this day our daily bread. And forgive us our debts, as we forgive our debtors. And lead us not into temptation, but deliver us from evil: For thine is the kingdom, and the power, and the glory, for ever. Amen* (Matthew 6:9-13).

Elisha called fire from Heaven at the time for evening prayer. Peter and James ascended the road to the Temple at the "hour of prayer" and saw the miraculous healing of the lame man. In Acts 4 the apostles prayed, the place was shaken, and everybody was filled with the Holy Ghost. Through these biblical examples, much of my life has been formed by the Master and my practice of prayer.

I was raised in the home of an old-time Pentecostal preacher. At our house, we prayed. Mom was blessed with one of those booming prayer voices. When Mom prayed, kids repented. She led countless ladies' prayer meetings and taught other ladies to pray. At church Mom prayed without ceasing, and she prayed loudly!

Dad always felt that the best prayer meetings were at 5 AM regardless of the time of year. To him my adolescent attendance would make the difference in the meeting, so he awakened me and shuttled us to the prayer meeting. My protests fell on uncaring ears. Even when Dad and I were the only ones in attendance, we prayed. Simply put, we prayed.

Church services always had pre-service prayer. We were there for the pre-pre-service prayer, stayed beyond the altar prayer time, and many nights were the last to leave the post-service prayer.

Somewhere I began to hunger for God. His calling was upon my life, but I found my own hunger. My prayers began to translate into a keen spiritual sensitivity. During one formative season, I was frustrated when I did not have opportunity for pulpit time, so I prayed and saw a most unusual phenomenon unfold. For over one year I stood behind the pulpit seldom but spent much time in the prayer room. During those months God began to speak, and week after week I would have my Bible open in the service to whatever passage God had impressed upon me. When the minister gave his text for his sermon, my Bible was already turned to the passage. God whispered to me the very things He gave to the ministers tasked with speaking.

In these forty years of full-time ministry, Tracie and I encountered many situations in which we found no choice but to pray. When we felt opposition, we agreed that we were on the same team and our answers were to be found in prayer. Many nights we lay side by side in our bed, holding hands and praying. We prayed over our children. We prayed over our finances. We prayed over Conroe Church. Never once did we see the protection and provision of God fail in our lives.

I became burdened for a young man who had drifted from the Lord. I only knew to pray for him. In prayer I felt myself move into a season of intercessory prayer for him. I prayed until I placed myself between him and a bad decision. That night I rejoiced and was quite surprised when the young man walked into the service and never stopped until he had knelt at the altar.

After a particularly stressful day, a visiting minister prophesied over Tracie and me. We were sitting together in a Shoney's restaurant when he began to speak. Then he reached across the table and laid hands on both of us and prayed. He prophesied that a seventy-five-soul revival for Conroe Church would begin that week. The revival of out-pouring began before the week's end, and to this day many of those seventy-five souls worship with us.

For us, prayer was not a program or just a discipline; it was a way of life. Prayer was part of our formative culture. God worked and answered many prayers. He did his part, but it was up to us to continue faithfully in prayer.

My dependency upon divine intervention led me a little further. I journeyed into what was known as "praying in the Holy Ghost"; that is, praying until I left my earthly realm to spend time with the Lord, speaking or praying in tongues. I began to marvel at the power of such prayer. *But ye, beloved, building up yourselves on your most holy faith, praying in the Holy Ghost* (Jude 20).

Praying in the Holy Ghost became a special place of refuge and intercession for me. Literally, I would pray until English left and the language of the Holy Ghost would emanate from my being. I experienced what Jesus spoke of in John 7. *He that believeth on me, as the scripture hath said, out of his belly shall flow rivers of living water* (John 7:38).

When I felt little or no faith, faith flowed from those prayers in the Holy Ghost. When I was discouraged, those prayers in the Holy Ghost built my faith. In a very substantial way, praying in tongues or praying in the Holy Ghost brought fresh life and miracles.

My son, Trent, had a growth the size and shape of a man's thumb appear on his tongue when he was nine years old. Understandably, we feared for him. I had already seen the hand of God upon his life. That big, black tumor on his tongue was a visible challenge to my faith. Our doctor said that a black tumor like this was most certainly malignant. Fear assaulted us. The enemy told me that the boy would lose his tongue or part of it and would never preach. I did what I knew to do. I prayed.

When the tumor was removed, the doctor brought it to us in a jar and said that without doubt it would come back from the pathologist with the diagnosis of malignant cancer. He urged us to prepare ourselves for the upcoming ordeal. Our process of preparation was to do the only thing we knew to do. We prayed. When the phone rang with the pathology report two weeks later, we were told the biopsy was benign. There was no cancer!

We prayed and God answered. The following Sunday night Trent preached his first sermon, "He Is Still God," to Conroe Church. To this day we rejoice in confidence that, notwithstanding the circumstance, God will take care of it. Our part of the formative process of such miraculous occurences was simply to pray.

In 1992 Conroe Church was only two years old, and we needed a building. So we prayed. We found a building we could convert to a church, so we prayed. In four weeks, our bank account increased from zero to almost one hundred thousand dollars. We kept praying. No bank would loan to us because we could not produce three years of financial records, so we prayed.

Then one day a pickup pulled up, and an old country guy, whom I would later know as John, got out and wanted to see our building. He walked through it, went back to his truck, and said before he closed the door, "Okay. Meet me at the bank, and I will loan you the money."

We had prayed, and God sent us a private investor who loaned us enough money to complete the project! As our new partner drove away that day, I asked, "Did anyone catch that man's name?" Our prayers were heard. I learned that God might just answer our named prayer request with an unnamed resource.

I understand that I am writing about the discipline of prayer. But to our way of living, prayer was no discipline. Prayer was the lifeline, our umbilical cord. Prayer was our manner of living. Prayer was and continues to be the only source of power that transports us from our limited, earthly realm into the Holy of Holies. *The earnest (heartfelt, continued) prayer of a righteous man makes tremendous power available [dynamic in its working]* (James 5:16, AMP).

I am not writing as an expert of all the theological parameters of prayer. I stake very little claim to the extensive exegesis of every verse in my King James Bible concerning this discipline. I merely grasp and refuse to let go of the simple reality that prayer is the most effective resource under heaven that can move heaven and change earth.

The day I received the phone call that my daughter could not find her baby, I prayed. When the baby was found face-down in the ditch in front of our house, unresponsive, we prayed. When I slipped into the emergency room and laid my hands on her little fifteen-month-old head, I prayed.

When the life flight doctor asked, "Who the *!@#%^ are you?" I prayed and replied, "I am her grandfather. You work on her body; I will work on her spirit." And I prayed.

As we drove beneath the helicopter, we prayed. We looked up to our baby but beyond her to our faithful God and prayed. Three hundred-plus people gathered with us in the waiting room of the trauma hospital and prayed. I stood beside her bed with her mommy and daddy and prayed.

For thirty hours, I prayed. When the trauma doctors told us that when the pressure on her little brain grew too great from the fluids being pumped into her innocent body, blood would come from her nose. They said that would tell us our baby had passed, so I prayed. When I saw those blood trickles run from her angel face and the machines cease making noise, I prayed. I prayed as Redonia held her baby, bathed her, and handed her to the nurse. My family walked down the world's longest hospital hallway, leaving our baby, and I prayed.

When three thousand-plus friends gathered at Conroe Church to pay respects to a fifteen-month-old baby girl and her family, I prayed. With fifteen hundred in the sanctuary as we attended a funeral no one wanted to attend, I prayed.

Formed

I prayed at the graveside that day. The next day at the graveside, I prayed. And the next day too, I prayed. I prayed the next day again. And again, I prayed. Now years later, I pray.

Whether our baby (and our other five grandchildren) live in heaven or on earth, . . . I pray.

The Discipline of Fasting

Fasting might be best known as the forsaken discipline. For me fasting is the least desirable or practiced of all the disciplines. I do not like to be hungry. I often tell others that I can begin a fast before breakfast and hear from God before lunch!

Scripture mentions fasting or the forfeiture of food more than eighty times. The significant themes of scriptural fasting center around a pursuit for direction or an answer from God, brokenness, grief, mourning, or even desperation for a godly intervention.

While biblical believers held fasting as a common practice, today's believers seldom practice regular fasting for kingdom purposes. Kingdom fasting seems to have been exchanged for vanity and fleshly purposes. Fasting for the purpose of weight loss or health benefits finds acceptance while fasting to deny oneself nutrition for the sake of drawing close to God wanes.

Intermittent fasting has become an industry. Weight loss and medical professionals encourage such to enhance healthy living while even the church seems to have set aside the value of fasting for the sake of heavenly life. Biblical fasting always focuses upon kingdom matters.

Much of modern Christianity has offered criticism of Catholicism and its practice of fasting certain things during the annual period of Lent, only to have embraced much the same practices when or if they fast. The Catholic might fast meat, drink, or some activity for the sake of his faith. In the same vein, some modern Christians practice "designer" fasting, forgoing such things as technology or social media, and applaud themselves over the great denial of such things. While these things are not wasted, the practice of fasting has become diluted by the setting aside of a narrow area of habits or appetites for a season.

A quick note reminds us of Jesus' admonition that fasting should be done in secret or privacy. Today's social-media culture seems to mandate a public declaration when one embarks upon a fast. *The Message* transliteration shares these words of our Lord: *When you practice some appetite-denying discipline to better concentrate on God, don't make a production out of it. It might turn you into a small-time celebrity but it won't make you a saint* (Matthew 6:18).

The Daniel fast has become popular over the last several years. I offer no criticism to those who endeavor to follow the practices of Daniel and his fellow prisoners. However, one must acknowledge the Daniel fast is an expensive endeavor to eat differently for a few days. The faster never gets hungry. I have often listened to the complaints of those embarking upon this fast of how expensive it is. Somehow, to my thought process spending more to eat less and then to call it a fast requires quite creative faith. I do understand, though, that no such endeavors to fast are unheeded by the Lord.

For the most part, biblical fasting portrays the setting aside of all foods for a designated number of days, drinking only water. When Jesus came from the wilderness and His fast of forty days, the King James Bible says, "He afterward hungered." Another reference indicates "He ate nothing."

The Discipline of Fasting

We discover examples in the Old Testament of the people's being called to solemn assemblies, where all were requested to fast. Such was the case in Joel 2:15 when the king called for solidarity in fasting as the nation faced invasion. They needed to invite the intervention of the Almighty!

Corporate fasting is an excellent avenue for the local church to come together in unity. Twice each year Conroe Church observes a season of prayer and fasting. We begin the year with twenty-one days of prayer and fasting. In this designated set of days, we seek the Lord and employ self-denial. In September we corporately participate in a week of sacrifice, including an organized corporate fast. We choose to allow people to fast in any number of ways. At times we encourage relinquishing media, something personal, or food. We have come to celebrate this discipline as a practice that produces incredible results in the days following.

I think it necessary to point out that fasting will not leverage God to your point of view. We do not fast to be blessed. I once heard a minister state he had just finished fasting for forty-one days, "One day longer than Jesus!"

More than once I counseled good church members who had fasted for extended periods of time and were unable to maintain their responsibilities. I insisted they break their fasts to gain nourishment for the sake of their jobs and families. Fasting does not buy our answer from God. Fasting does, however, produce in us a brokenness before God.

Fasting cannot be for others or even for God. As with all the disciplines, fasting is a gift we give ourselves. When we fast, we declare our humility and even dependence upon God. Fasting helps us be more broken and open before the Lord. It breaks and prepares us for God's will in our lives.

We had arrived at a transitional point in our young ministry. We were happily employed at a nice church, living in a very nice parsonage with a significant and respected pastor, when God spoke to my heart. I knew transition was coming. God would soon move us.

God said, "Fast," and I did so for three days. This was total fasting—no food, no coffee, just water. I prepared to break the fast at the end of the third day when God said, "Not yet." So I did not eat and continued to fast for another five days. At the end of that interval, I finished praying for my soup and picked up my spoon. Immediately, the telephone rang.

That call was equal to Paul's Macedonian call. As I broke my fast, I received my "Conronian" call. We came and planted Conroe Church in 1990. Our faith has never wavered, nor have we ever considered leaving our calling. For we know that God called us clearly. His call to us to Conroe was greatly reinforced in our hearts because the call came in the instant we broke that season of fasting. We desired to be sensitive to the Spirit, humble before God, and ready for whatever transition He had planned for us.

Foster stated, "Fasting reveals the things that control us." This is evidenced by the things that surface as we endeavor to practice this discipline. Pride, resentment, anger, and even lust are often revealed when we set to fast, depriving ourselves of food, drink, and other things with which we cover our inner persons. While we might rationalize our behaviors during a fast as a product of food deprivation, one must realize the things revealed in our flesh while fasting really manifest the spirits we have entertained rather than the lack of food content in our bellies.

The Discipline of Fasting

Indeed, fasting is the discipline we can easily ignore, but it produces the greatest benefits of humility and brokenness before God. Fasting is not a requirement for salvation, but fasting is a tremendous discipline that, when practiced with the right motive, will not just help keep you saved but indeed might just help you to embrace less of yourself and more of our Lord.

The Discipline of Study

Study of the Word of God is another discipline that transforms us through the constant renewal of our minds. *And be not conformed to this world: but be ye transformed by the renewing of your mind, that ye may prove what is that good, and acceptable, and perfect, will of God* (Romans 12:2). As we study the Word of God daily, we bring our inner man to the place of daily attention to the things of God.

There is life in the Word. The literal *logos* (the divine expression) is the essence of God. *In the beginning was the Word, and the Word was with God, and the Word was God* (John 1:1).

While I chronicle my journey of spiritual formation, I have shared and will share anecdotal and personal references that have made great contributions to my development. The following is one of my starkest personal illustrations.

I attended first grade at Southmayd Elementary on Lawndale Street in Houston, Texas, the city where my father attended Texas Bible College. My mother worked a secular job and looked after her three children. Though compassionate, Mom was formidably tough.

The day my teacher called Mom to the school for a parent-teacher meeting is burned deeply into my psyche. On a Friday in 1967, I saw Mom come into the classroom. Apparently, my teacher had communicated with my mother that I was failing to read and falling behind the rest of the class. This did not bode well for her eldest son, me.

Mom's name is Joye, and I like to say that the "J" in Joye stands for Gibraltar. Joye "Gibraltar" Smith woke me the next morning with these fearsome words: "Kent, today you will read." The problem was, of course, that Kent could not read yet.

She sat me at the kitchen table, opened her Bible to John 1:1, and said, "Start copying this!"

I began to copy these words: "In the beginning was the Word, and the Word was with God, and the Word was God." I wrote with my jumbo pencil on my Big Chief tablet again, "In the beginning was the Word, and the Word was with God, and the Word was God." Again and again.

Gibraltar said, "Okay, do the next one," and I wrote, "The same was in the beginning with God." Again and again.

"Next," came the commandment from the fearsome rock, and I dutifully wrote, "All things were made by him; and without him was not any thing made that was made." Again and again.

"That's good, keep going."

I licked my pencil and wrote, "In him was life; and the life was the light of men." Yes, again and again.

By verse five I was reading! "And the light shineth in darkness; and the darkness comprehended it not."

What I read later that day, *And the Word was made flesh, and dwelt among us, (and we beheld his glory, the glory as of the only begotten of the Father,) full of grace and truth*, burned this event into my spirit. My discovery that day was more than reading; rather, my learning to read in this manner implanted a cognizance of God's very nature. This formative moment remains unequaled in my memory.

The Discipline of Study

A single Saturday's study had produced a love for reading, a hunger for study, and revelatory truth that is with me to this day! I still stand in awe that my first day of reading comprehension included the certain reality that God understands humanity. For all I knew at the time, He probably lived in the same apartment complex as my family!

I could certainly write more concerning the analytics of study. I could share more scriptural absolutes and biblical references concerning the importance of study for the sake of the approval of others and of God. Instead, I chose the experiential aspect of disciplined study. That day of study established truths deep inside me that remain settled more than fifty years later.

The discipline of study for me has entailed digging deeply into a single verse, text, or even phrase, then comparing the King James text to other trusted translations. I can then apply the freshly acquired revelation to the procedures of normal life. For there is life in the Word of God. Just as the creative word formed the heavens and the earth, so does the living Word bring life to lifeless things.

Truth matters! Absolute truth matters absolutely. Although living in the Spirit requires the effects of experience, experience alone does not a discipline make. There must be a fusion of the Spirit of God and the truth of God. Such is found when one gifts to himself the discipline of study.

God is a Spirit: and they that worship him must worship him in spirit and in truth (John 4:24). The pursuit of spirit and truth mandates developing a love for truth. Hence, we discover Paul's admonition for receiving such a love. *Whose coming is after the working of Satan . . . and with all deceivableness of unrighteousness in them that perish;*

because they received not the love of the truth, that they might be saved (2 Thessalonians 2:9-10).

Then comes the responsibility of separating truth from error. Study divides error from truth. Indeed, spirits of error are dispatched to subvert the spirit of truth. *We are of God: he that knoweth God heareth us; he that is not of God heareth not us. Hereby know we the spirit of truth, and the spirit of error* (1 John 4:6).

Paul's pastoral admonition to the young Timothy profoundly yet clearly outlines the responsibility of the discipline of study:

> *Study and be eager and do your utmost to present yourself to God approved (tested by trial), a workman who has no cause to be ashamed, correctly analyzing and accurately dividing [rightly handling and skillfully teaching] the Word of Truth* (2 Timothy 2:15, AMP).

This segment is roughly one thousand words long. If the significance of study cannot be conveyed in that span, no lengthy prose or pontification can transmit the value of gifting oneself the discipline of study.

The Discipline of Simplicity

Simplicity is a discipline revealing an inward reality that results in an outward manifestation. Paul emphasized this simplicity with a single word, "moderation." *Let your moderation be known unto all men. The Lord is at hand* (Philippians 4:5).

The discipline of simplicity produces honesty, modesty, and generosity of living that is divorced from the lust for status or position. Our modern social constructs often create new cultures within themselves that are complicated with the strife of human interaction.

An old bishop told the story of a man marooned on a deserted island. When rescuers came ashore, they inquired about the three huts they saw on the hillside. The solitary man replied, "The first hut is my house. The second hut is my church. The third hut is where I used to go to church!"

Such is how human interaction becomes complicated. This marooned man was the only member of his church and still had to change churches.

We complicate the most beautiful creations of God by our need for human government. This is reflected by the simplest of relationships, two children on the playground. Pretty soon one will be bossing the other around. Human interaction prompts human government (or even church government). Human government always declines into human politics and the erosion of the pure simplicity God so desires in us and our relationships.

In the beginning, God's creation was simple until a single, inharmonious voice was given heed. In a single day, simplicity was replaced with confusion, chaos, and division, resulting in the eventual competition between brothers and the tragic death of one brother at the hand of the other. All flowed from the confusion allowed into the simplicity of a worship service.

Our human nature is rife with human desires. Materialism is a core doctrine of our free-choice culture. We want more and more stuff. On the other hand, Jesus taught: *But seek ye first the kingdom of God, and his righteousness; and all these things shall be added unto you* (Matthew 6:33).

We complicate our human experience with our humanity. We allow far too much fleshly manipulation into what God desired to be so simple. This verse assures us that if we seek the simple things of God, He will add to our lives all the stuff we could want or desire.

When Israel wanted a king like other nations, God felt disappointment in their longing for an earthly kingdom. His plan for them was a simple, heavenly one. Just as Israel begged for King Saul, one day they would plead for relief from the complicated tyranny of human will.

My daily drive carried me through a rural intersection we called "the Y." In the middle of the intersection stood single, skinny cow, occupying a barbed-wire farm lot. Each day I marveled as the bovine strained her neck through the strands of wire and pushed for the weeds outside the fence. Then came the day I saw that she had finally been granted her wish and was in the roadside ditch, straining against the same barbed wire she fought yesterday on the other side. Now she wished she was inside the fence.

Such is our human experience. We have been granted a simple, safe reality, but we press for things outside the planned simplicity God has for us. Far too often we, like my bovine friend, attain what we wanted but wish we had not traded what we had.

Foster wrote, "Asceticism and simplicity are mutually incompatible." The discipline of simplicity does not renounce possessions; rather, it holds the correct perspective of possessions. Money is not the root of all evil; the love of money is the evil root. God has no problem with our being blessed. Issues arise when we appreciate our blessings much more than we appreciate the One who blesses.

Paul wrote of this failure in human experience. *Who changed the truth of God into a lie, and worshipped and served the creature more than the Creator, who is blessed for ever* (Romans 1:25).

Too often we expect the kingdom of God to be patterned after our American free-enterprise culture. We construct concepts of material prosperity and interpret God's blessing as validation of us. This should not be! We should never elevate the created blessings over our blessed Creator.

Simplicity keeps us focused. Moderation allows us to walk through life with the abundance of the Creator and His created things and to keep them in perspective on the way.

God has blessed Tracie and me with more than we deserve. He also has blessed us by not granting us all that we have asked for. Our home is beautiful. Our cars are nice. Our wardrobes are moderate. Yet after forty years of marriage, we have acquired little beyond what you see in our daily life. Our trophies are the many souls God has given our ministry. Our possessions are in direct correlation with the workings of God in our lives. We know that our golden years will be filled with the same provision we have enjoyed for a lifetime. We have endeavored to pursue the discipline of simplicity these years. Our most fervent desires have been for the blessing of Conroe Church, and the reality is Conroe Church has been a greater blessing to us than we to them.

Moderation has been a core teaching at Conroe Church. Pride is the chief enemy of simplicity. I have insisted that Conroe Church will not be the best, the biggest, the greatest of all churches—though I feel it is. However, a claim of "the best" requires the comparison of oneself to all others. This is a trap to prevent us from attaining simplicity.

One should never be like the Pharisee, who compared himself to the publican and thanked God he was not like that guy. Jesus responded that the humble attitude obtained the favor of God. The simplicity of a penitent publican trumps the pride of the praying Pharisee every time.

When we set aside the pursuit of simplicity, we risk acquiring addictive behaviors. There is not greater example of this today than the culture of social media. How and why did it become important for us to post a picture of the expensive restaurants we visit and never the take-out pizza from the night before? We post selfies when we dress up but not the pictures taken while cleaning our homes. We self-congratulate our service to others. We brag (in the language of being blessed) of things we possess and do. We even post the great things occurring at church and the important people who visited but never about the family who chose to change churches or filed bankruptcy. We exaggerate our blessings as a validation to feel as relevant as the others who exaggerate their blessings. Surreality has replaced simplicity!

The Discipline of Simplicity

Had the good Samaritan had a smart phone and social media account, he could have live-streamed himself parking his donkey and looking over the poor wounded man. He might have made sure to get a good shot of his pouring oil in the wounds of the man before he ceremoniously picked up the guy and placed him strategically for the camera in the back of his seventy-five-thousand-dollar SUV. Maybe he would have driven him to the Salvation Army shelter for the homeless and captioned the video, "So Blessed!"

Instead, this good man quietly looked after the needs of the wounded man and got him the help he needed, using his own money. We never learned his name. However, we did gain a snapshot of a selfless man who had discovered the discipline of simplicity.

The Discipline of Solitude

Solitude is self-awareness of an inner fulfilment. Having such assurance might mean that you will be alone, but you are not by yourself!

I have acquaintances who are terrified of being alone. They are not happy outside a crowd. Their survival depends upon the flock. But the eagle soars high above the noise of the barnyard, escaping the mundane chaos of the many. The eagle soars alone.

Solitude is to be treasured rather than escaped. As a leader, I have attended meetings, sitting alone and feeling alone amid the crowd, but never have I been lonely. Somewhere in this life of ministry, I had to develop a contentment within myself and with God. Like all positions of leadership, ministry does get lonely, but the minister does not have to be alone. In moments of solitude, meditation can flow without the hindrance of surrounding clamor.

Jesus exampled to us the discipline of solitude when He left the crowd and spent forty days in the wilderness. He emerged with power and demonstrated His divine nature. Our Lord often retreated to the hills or mountain to be alone. On His last night in the garden before his betrayal, He "was withdrawn from them" to pray.

Aloneness creates an environment for special communication with the Master. While no man should set himself apart as an island, great things emerge from our seeking solitude with the Lord.

We need community. Paul instructed us not to forsake our coming together. Family and fellowship are disciplines that should not be avoided. We need each other. Parents need their children, and children need their parents. Humanity needs humanity. Great strength is gained when we share life with others. Our personal growth can seldom outgrow our relationship with others. However, we should not substitute our need for solitude with self and God with a constant clamor of party and fellowship.

Tracie and I take two vacations every year. We leave town and go off alone. This retreat has become important to our marriage and makes us better pastors. Retreating into solitude brings strength and renewal. After a few days away, we are filled with restorative strength and faith. When we return home, we are refreshed and renewed.

I often tell leaders they must recreate before they can re-create. Solitude with God prepares us for the next thing God has planned in our lives.

Fifteen months after the loss of our granddaughter, we left on a road trip for more than three weeks. We had no planned destination. We refused to visit a chain restaurant except for a daily ice-cream cone from McDonalds. One of those days was spent on a Florida beach. I hate beaches. That year, though, I fell in love with sand and sea.

There I was, the Pentecostal preacher—in my long-sleeved white shirt, Sheaves for Christ ball cap, and my long britches rolled up—sitting on the beach alone. Alone but not alone. Amid the roar of crashing water, the taste of salty wind, the feeling of grit between my toes, and the sight of Tracie as she waded in the surf, I felt the uplift of solitude. The wind blew, and God spoke refreshing healing into my spirit in my silence. The experience was so profound that I purposed to repeat it the next day and every day until our travel resumed. I returned to that site two years later and again rejoiced in the solitude.

Another Christmas we traveled to Wyoming and for a week traversed park roads, marveling at snow, animals, and silence. This year I plan to seek more solitude in South Dakota, for in the solitude of silence, I find the re-creative power of recreation.

The preacher of Ecclesiastes insisted that there is an time for absolute silence. The voice of Zacharias was silenced for the entire pregnancy of Elisabeth. Imagine what transpired in the silence of that season of his life.

My friend Foster wrote, "If we are silent when we should speak or we speak when we should be silent, we are not living the discipline of solitude or silence." Eremitism is not disciplined solitude. Hermitism provides little spiritual profit. Monkism is not a path to sainthood. Monasticism has no compulsive spiritual requirements. Solitude, however, is a spiritual discipline well worth pursuing.

As I write this, I sit at the conference table in my office, surrounded by our pastoral staff as they plan events for the next month. The conversation is noisy and clamorous by nature. I sit in the middle of this clamor and have escaped into that place of solitude where God whispers to me. I know that the events being planned around me will be wonderful but will not compare to the solitude that facilitates communion with God.

Our family had gathered in San Francisco for the wedding of a nephew. One day everyone but me was busy with wedding stuff, so I caught a cab to the Golden Gate

Bridge. I wandered through the park and the visitor center. I marveled at the incredible masterpiece of architecture that has stood as a national treasure for so many years. Then I walked the 8981-foot length and back, 1.7 miles each way. I took 11, 975 steps that afternoon, surrounded by others but in deep solitude with my Creator. I walked and God whispered. Even when the bicycle guy hit me, my solitude with the Master went uninterrupted. When asked by a family member later that day, "You really walked that bridge? Why would you do that?" I smiled, remembering the wonder of the moments of silence and solitude.

The power of solitude has been instrumental in my spiritual formation. Being secure amid solitude has provided great boldness for me when standing before large groups. I understand that solitude provides a solace able to liberate one from the control of the crowd.

Listen to those who speak publicly. Compare the man who speaks boisterously with the one who speaks quietly and powerfully. The noise of the clamor is long subsided, yet one feasts upon the depth of the still, quiet voice cultivated in solitude and in the presence of the Master.

I admit I love the moments of great spiritual breakthroughs. Miraculous moments inspire my faith to no end. Yet seeking silence and solitude provides more strength for the journey than clamoring crowds can ever comprehend.

The Discipline of Submission

Submission is a most misunderstood discipline. Both believers and non-believers recoil and even resist when the word "submission" arises. We seem to have no problem with submission as long as it applies to someone else.

Foster wrote, "The moment we make a discipline our central focus, we turn it into a law. Hence the freedoms found in the discipline are lost." Paul wrote similarly to the Corinthians: *All things are lawful unto me, but all things are not expedient: all things are lawful for me, but I will not be brought under the power of any* (1 Corinthians 6:12).

Overemphasis on any discipline creates an opportunity for legalism. If the goal of the discipline is fasting, fasting becomes the object rather than the freedom and purpose of the discipline. The same happens when the act of submission is emphasized more than the fruit of submission.

Jesus made an eye from mud, but the method of the miracle cannot be emphasized more than the miracle itself. There was a great work done on the cross at Calvary, but some have endeavored to sell slivers of wood, claiming them be actual pieces of the cross. The physical cross contained nothing healing or salvific; instead, the cross was part of God's method to buy salvation for each of us.

Such is the same with the practice of submission. Those who demand submission are not worthy of it. However, each of us is required to offer submission. Submission is not to be offered from a wife to a husband only, but a husband offers submission to his wife as well. For some, discipline has become a legal tool, the spirit of submission having been missed. Paul wrote of this mutual submission in Ephesians. *Submitting yourselves one to another in the fear of God* (Ephesians 5:21).

Submission is a two-way street, and overemphasis of submission can create a painful way of life. Yet the lack of emphasis on submission allows for rebellion and other unhealthy spiritual conditions.

The practice of tithe is really the pursuit of submission. One places his life and finances under submission to the Master. As a pastor I have been tempted to teach eternal judgment to those who have struggled with tithing. Such preaching might create a compliance with the teaching, but the spirit of the discipline would be missed completely.

Submission provides freedom to the one who tithes. His submission opens the windows of heaven for God to bless that tithe beyond expectation. A tithe that is only obedient or compliant seems to miss the wonder of a tithe that comes from submission.

Foster continues, "Most of us have been exposed to such a mutilated form of biblical submission that either we have embraced the deformity or have altogether rejected the Discipline." Too often leaders have demanded the brand of submission that can never compare to a spirit of submission.

Jesus, the perfect Lamb sacrificed from the foundation of the earth, submitted to baptism by John the Baptist. The sinless Creator submitted Himself. Our Lord also submitted to the shame of the cross when He could have called upon the heavenly hosts to deliver Him from that painful and degrading process.

Submission is not a denial of self. One does not check in his personality and other privileges at the door of submission. Submission in not the doormat of equal rights. In all reality, the submitted person is oftentimes greater than the one submitted to. Submission creates its own power over the issue at play in submission.

I was once called by my leadership into a most uncomfortable meeting. While I had remained in compliance with a policy, someone else had not. The spirit of the meeting was a bit abusive, and my leadership asked me to submit to an inequitable decision that forced submission from me but no one else. During the meeting, one of my leaders said he wanted us to pray that I would be okay with the decision. My human spirit flared; I wanted to set the dumpster on fire! Instead, I agreed to prayer and prophesied to the leader that this would present itself again in less than three months. I then turned and knelt before the two men for them to pray for me. Submission is not always easy.

Three months later in a public meeting, an innocent party requested prayer for the very things I had prophesied. God publicly revealed the erroneous and unreasonable demands and vindicated me publicly. Submitting three months earlier had not been easy, but submission is always right.

I have chosen this personal example, for how can one comment upon the issues of submission when he has not passed the submission test in a very uncomfortable situation? Submission transacts when one submits to things he does not agree with. Submission is not cooperation or simple compliance. Submission is accepting what is not easy and maintaining right standing with man and God during the process. The byproduct of such a decision is the power produced by submission. In that most awkward and uncomfortable act of submission, God granted me great favor moving forward in that circumstance.

We are to walk boldly through this life with the confidence of the Holy Ghost. While we should walk in humility, we are not required to check in our self-assurance. We confidently accept that God has made each of with unique strengths and idiosyncrasies. We are not required to be doormats for others. The same God who gave us these traits also allows opportunities so that we may humble ourselves and submit to others lesser than we, who quite frankly are not worthy of that submission. Then God grants us new giftings when we choose to respond correctly with submission to those unwarranted circumstances.

The discipline of submission is a gift to oneself that must be purchased from the low shelves of life. Face it, we like the gifts that are prominent and desirable. Forty years ago, I sat in a Bible-school class and listened to an elder. He entreated us to see that the greatest blessings of life are not prominently displayed on the high shelves within view of all. He explained the greatest gifts are on the bottom shelves and require you to get on your knees to reach deep for them.

Submission is not a top-shelf gift. Submission requires you to be willing to get on your knees, reach deep, maybe bury your face in the carpet, and strain to reach those places low enough where God has hidden His best gifts.

Jesus exemplified this in the garden when He struggled with submission to the cross. *He went away again the second time, and prayed, saying, O my Father, if this cup may not pass away from me, except I drink it, thy will be done* (Matthew 26:42).

The Discipline of Submission

Submission is the most powerful of discipline gifts. Others might humble you, others may punish you, but no one can force your submission. When you submit, you allow the best of yourself to be yielded to another. You give your best when you give your submission. When submitted, you give the gift of yourself to the one submitted to. You give the gift of yourself to God. But the greatest recipient of all is yourself. When you give your submission to others, you give the gift of freedom to yourself!

The Discipline of Service

Service is a gift wrapped entirely in our choices. Foster wrote, "Service enables us to say, 'no!' " Daily, each of us are presented with this same choice. We can say, "Yes," to the menial service of others. Saying, "No" to the service of others is a de facto "yes" to the serving of ourselves.

We live in a culture of the social-media post or "me" time. The need for "me" time fails to acknowledge that real peace and strength do not come from "me" time but are invariably found in "others" time. The discipline of serving stands alone in the disciplines, for it more than any other completely removes the question, "What is in it for me?"

Ginger came into our lives nearly thirty years ago. She volunteered at our Christian school for eighteen years, serving selflessly. Her husband would sometimes say it was time for her to stop serving, but she would pray and continue serving. Hundreds of toddlers carried on her hips learned phonics while she taught and served a generation of little people. To this day, I meet young adults around our community who were in her class, and the first question is, "How is Sis. Ginger?" Thousands of times I have seen a crying toddler lift little arms and say, "Ginga." With a tired but happy face, she picked him up, placed him on her hip, and moved to her next act of service.

Then Conroe Christian School closed, and Ginger came to us broken. She inquired, "Pastor, where am I going to serve now?"

Fumbling for words, I simply said, "Ginger, let's pray about it and see what doors God opens." I know, this is a great spiritual way to say, "Beats me, too." But we did pray.

A few days later an animated Ginger came by. "I have found my place to serve!" She then began to share a story of prayer and God's direction for her next place of service. "I am to clean the church!"

Huh?

She continued, "For eighteen years I have served my church and my pastor in that preschool classroom, and now I am going to serve my church and pastor by cleaning the church two times every week!"

That was ten years ago. Today she still cleans Conroe Church, serving her pastor and the Lord. She does not realize that she also serves hundreds of other people who have never had to use an unkept restroom or drink from a dirty water fountain. She has never asked for supplies. If the office fails to keep adequate supplies, she just brings her own and never says a word. Ginger is my master when it comes to living the discipline of service.

Jesus was the ultimate servant leader long before all the modern authors wrote books on the subject. Seldom a week goes by that I do not reference His servant leadership.

The day Jesus determined "he must needs go through Samaria," the disciples no doubt thought in terms of political and prejudicial implications. Most Jews would travel around Samaria rather than step into the area. But Jesus announced, in essence, "I am not bypassing Samaria, nor am I going through Samaria. I must go *to* Samaria." We discover that upon His arrival He kept a divine appointment with the least likely of ladies.

The Discipline of Service

Following the Last Supper, Jesus rose, wrapped the towel of service around His waist, and became the servant to the disciples who would serve Him until their own deaths. This group of men had been known to argue about who was the greatest among them, but they had to permit the One, who they all knew was indeed the greatest, to serve them! *And he sat down, and called the twelve, and saith unto them, If any man desire to be first, the same shall be last of all, and servant of all* (Mark 9:35).

Too often we choose a path of service that is as self-serving as it is serving others. How often have you seen someone list all the things he has been tasked to do for "those poor people"? Social media again reveals the motives of our service when we are obligated to post selfies of our benevolent acts. Politicians arrive with their entourage and video team to a food bank and hand a single bag of groceries to a single person in line. Meanwhile, cameras record, voice-over commentary is planned, and photographers shout, "Hold still for a minute when you hand her the sack!" I marvel when the children of aging parents post pictures of themselves with the long description of all "they are so blessed" to do for their parents, when in fact the public act of service was more self-serving than parent-serving.

Contrast this with the servant who has chosen the invisible pathway of service. His name need not be called. His service need not be recognized publicly. But he serves selflessly and faithfully when all others have yet to arrive or have left the premises long ago.

Tracie has a friend whom I will refer to as Friend. Friend truly has excelled in the service of others. She finds ways to involve herself in the ministries and projects of everybody. When Tracie and I arrive at an event, Friend got there yesterday just to make sure the event had all the help it needed. When Tracie and I leave, we will inevitably see Friend selflessly finishing some act of service for the event that was left behind by the rest of us. I hold Friend in the highest of esteem. Friend has learned the secret of service to others that makes her greater than the rest of us.

I was handed a monogrammed towel during the ceremony of my ordination. That towel was to represent the role of servant in my ministry. Ministry is a perpetual act of service to others. More than once, I have been offended by the lowliness of some request; then I remember the towel.

My role and years of service have allowed me to be honored many times. Receiving such honor is always awkward, and I hope it continues to be so. When such awkwardness is lost, I fear a sense of entitlement may have crept upon me.

Conroe Church blesses us. If I try to vacuum, someone will take the vacuum from me because the culture of Conroe Church is to honor their pastor. Yet when I fail at least to attempt these menial tasks, I actually fail Conroe Church. I fail the Lord, and most sadly, I fail myself. For service to others is the engine of humility.

Somewhere I inherited Richard. He was an old, obnoxious man with little training in consideration of others. He lived alone in a shack in the woods and had attended Conroe Church for more than twenty years. His past failures had caused his family to ostracize him. Now in his mid-80s, he was alone, an aging, unclaimed member of society.

I visited him in the hospital when he totaled his vehicle by pulling onto the highway without looking. He was in much pain as I stood by his bedside. Then, in an instant, I inherited him. Richard opened the drawer beside the bed, handed me his keys and wallet, and said, "I can no longer drive or take care of myself!" Instantly, I was the proud new owner of a most difficult octogenarian! I had not been in the market for such a thing.

The next six months were a blur of challenge, humiliation, anger, and anguish. Before Richard left the hospital from his wreck, he was diagnosed with pancreatic cancer, and so began his journey into death and my own odyssey into serving someone I did not want to serve.

I began to manage his money and personal affairs. This included moving him from the shack in the woods into a senior care facility. While he contributed to the misery levels of fellow residents in a transitional care home, I fell to the process of dismantling his not-so-pretty life and his shack. I sorted through his meager belongings. I learned that he had lived in the shack for years with no plumbing. The place smelled of human feces and an unwashed body. The bedroom floor had long settled into the dirt, and a piece of plywood was its substitute. I gathered unwashed laundry and washed more than two hundred filthy pairs of underwear. The stench of his shack became the stench of Tracie's magazine-quality home.

For Richard's new apartment we purchased a bed, lift chair, and dinette. We furnished his kitchen with a single shopping venture to Walmart. The big move day resulted in more misery for us and complaints from my octogenarian. He went to Sunday lunch with us on Mother's Day that year. I took Tracie to a nice, little, girlish, tea-party restaurant, and my obnoxious octogenarian took out his false teeth, asked for somebody to clean them, and yelled rudely to the waitress for, "Coffee!"

I found my personal low spot the day Richard's suffering from the cancer caused his body to break out in hives. The only relief he could find was rubbing lotion on himself. But when the pain moved to his back and places of his body he could not reach, he looked to me. My initial reaction was: "This man of God is not doing this!" Behind his back as I rubbed lotion on the ornery legacy, I asked the Lord, "What is this all about?" The Lord was silent as I mutely suffered and served my non-compliant octogenarian.

I rationalized that this was but for a season. I knew that death was not far. As I rubbed lotion and wept before the Lord, I realized servants do not say, "No," to those they have said, "Yes," to serving.

Upon Richard's death and the final dissolution of his affairs, his life was reduced to a small file folder kept in an old briefcase in my garage. His family had told me not to inform them when he died. Conroe Church conducted a funeral for him. The funeral home took his remains to the veteran's cemetery. I was left with a relief from the season, unanswered questions, and a fresh revelation that service requires an immense amount of discipline and is the complete and absolute choice of the servant.

When Jesus chose to wrap Himself in the towel of service before His disciples, Peter resisted because he did not understand what compelled our Lord in that moment to serve them. Likewise, I can offer no explanation for the compelling I felt to serve Richard. Peter taught me to accept the service of the Lord that night. Richard taught me that if Jesus wrapped Himself in the servant's towel, so must I.

The Discipline of Confession

"Confession and forgiveness are realities that transform us," wrote my friend Foster. The discipline of confession is a conscious choice of action that allows us to grow into maturity as we allow our own vulnerabilities and failures to surface. This singular practice ushers us into the very presence of the Almighty. *Till we all come in the unity of the faith, and of the knowledge of the Son of God, unto a perfect man, unto the measure of the stature of the fulness of Christ* (Ephesians 4:13).

Our American culture makes us independent from everyone else when in all reality we must have each other. The trust we find in community aids us not to be intimidated to accept our own vulnerabilities and does not let us think that nobody is as sinful as we. James insisted within his exposition on healing prayer that we should confess our sins one to another. *Confess your faults one to another, and pray one for another, that ye may be healed. The effectual fervent prayer of a righteous man availeth much* (James 5:16).

In this one verse, James shared the secrets to the discipline of confession.

1. Confess your sins.
2. Receive the confession of sins.
3. Pray for each other.
4. Then the righteousness of the confessed person creates an effective prayer of forgiveness.

The secret ingredient for confession is forgiveness. Here is how it works. Sinner Guy #1 has been overtaken in a fault. His conscience bothers him, and he feels the need to offload these pressures. He goes to Guy #2 and shares his heart. Unbeknownst to Guy #1, Guy #2 had the same issue last year. So Sinner Guy #1 confesses to Sinner Guy #2. Now Sinner Guy #2 remembers his struggle and confesses to Sinner Guy #1 that he had the same struggle awhile back. Now both Sinner Guys know about the other. Both Guys agree to pray for each other that this never happens again.

Somewhere in the process, both Guys dropped the Sinner first name and now are just two Guys, two Guys who are praying together for each other. But their prayer has changed, for they both have found forgiveness. The weight of condemnation has been lifted. Both Guy #1 and Guy #2 have gained victory over their sin, and their prayers together have become more powerful and effective. Presto, two Sinner Guys are now two Powerful Prayer Guys!

The question arises, how can Guy #2 not have compassion on Guy #1? How can he not offer the compassion of understanding his friend's failure? How can he criticize or condemn his friend? How can he ignore the reality that all have sinned and fallen short? How can he, Guy #2, not keep Guy #1's confession in confidence? These questions provide a singular answer.

He who has been forgiven has the power to forgive! Forgiveness is the lubricant of confession. We confess and are forgiven. We are forgiven; thus, we forgive. We forgive the confession because we were forgiven when we confessed. We recognize that those we confess to are forgiven and understand the responsibility of forgiveness.

Forgiven people forgive! Hence, the discipline of confession is liberating. We both confess and receive confessions. We have been forgiven and we also forgive!

Jesus silently bent and wrote in the dust of Jerusalem when the morally failed young woman was thrown at His feet. When the world throws you away, where better to land than at Jesus' feet?

"Where are your accusers?"

Bewildered response: "It does not look like I have any." No denial of the accusation. A confession of silence which screamed, "Yes, I am guilty!"

God said, "I am not talking about this any more. It is a moot point. Man isn't accusing you, and neither am I!"

And we see the holiness of God, who her accusers no doubt understood knew of their unconfessed sins. Her accusers confessed by dropping the accusations and leaving. These men had the power to forgive her even before they threw her away.

The Creator of all things then said, "Go!"

Go? she wondered.

"Sin no more." In a single instant, Jesus showed us that man can forgive even before God forgives!

I was given the opportunity to mirror the Lord when He revealed to me the pre-marital consummation of wedlock. The engaged couple involved themselves with such every afternoon at their newly purchased home. Both young people were incredibly talented. Both loved God.

So I asked the Lord: "What would You do, Jesus?"

When He answered, I was shocked. "Forgive them."

"How, Lord?"

"Like I did."

"Not my job, Lord," I broached respectfully.

"Try it."

So I went to the pre-wedding consummators, and we talked. They were embarrassed. I was embarrassed. They wanted to know what I planned to do.

"I forgive you," I explained.

They looked baffled.

"I forgive you," I repeated. "Here is what happens. Both of you are forgiven. I will not remove you from your leadership positions. I know God forgives. I am forgiving you. From this time until your wedding, this activity ceases. I will ask you weekly how things are going, and I expect you to look me in the eye and say you are behaving. Therefore, I forgive you. Let's go forward, and you sin no more."

My forgiveness saved that couple—and my family. A few years later when my own daughter had a moral failure, church leaders stood and requested that I treat my child with the same mercy I had given theirs years before!

The forgiven are the best forgivers! The forgiven are the safest confessors!

Actually, in the English language "confessor" is both the sharer of confession and the receiver of confession.

> Confessors confess to confessors.
> Confessors forgive confessors.
> No confession, no forgiveness.
> No forgiveness, no confession.

Jesus said it perfectly, "Go, and sin no more."

What more can I say? Let me offer some practical advice. Be careful whom you invite into your business. Seek counsel from an elder saint of God or minister. God gives us pastors for times like these. Seasoned saints who have already walked this pathway are wonderful choices. Create a relationship of trust. Confess your sins. Let that person pray for you, and you pray for him or her. Pray together.

The young lady came to us, confessing her moral sin and pregnancy. I did not know what to do. When an elder lady was welcomed into the conversation, I witnessed compassion and forgiveness from that dear saint of God that astounded me. I would later learn that, many years ago, the dear, seasoned sister had been young and pregnant out of wedlock. She knew exactly how to forgive her new young friend. It seems the forgiven have learned both the power of confessing and the wonder of forgiveness. Those forgiven are the best forgivers!

The Discipline of Celebration

Celebration brings strength, hope, and life! The byproduct of purposeful celebration is the joy of the Lord.

Many times I have prayed with someone as he or she was filled with the gift of the Holy Ghost. Inevitably, when the Spirit enters, the seeker begins to speak in the heavenly language of the Spirit. As the new babe continues to pray and the Spirit manifests in him, I have witnessed a literal countenance change. At times it seems years of darkness leave his countenance. I have seen ladies I thought were in their middle years have a countenance change that seemed to take many years from their faces.

Accompanying this moment is realization by the new baby in Christ that old things have passed away, and he rejoices. An incredible display of joy will appear upon the countenance as he celebrates what God has done in his life. In that moment, those praying around the new believer also feel the uplift of faith in their own spirits. That is the moment the newly born convert celebrates and rejoices because he suddenly feels the joy of the Lord!

Last year I witnessed an older lady experience this. She came to church, and we would learn she had dealt with drug and alcohol addictions. She had spent many years in the penitentiary. She carried the marks and scars of sin, and her countenance was dark.

Then she was filled with the Holy Ghost! All at once, I saw the joy of the Lord come upon her. The darkness in her countenance left. I had started by praying for a sixty-plus-year-old lady, but in an instant, it seemed she was barely fifty years of age. She rejoiced and celebrated. For the next two years—until she moved to a new location—I marveled as she walked in the celebration of the newness of life.

Last Sunday at the end of our service, a dear sister came to me with news. Deadra had Facetimed her from her new church with a testimony.

Her husband was being led by the Lord to the church somewhat reluctantly. He really did not grasp the financial aspects of giving and tithing. During the service, the pastor called for an offering to be brought to the front, and the husband said, "Okay, God." As he laid his offering on the altar, he lifted his hands, the power of God fell upon him, and he was filled with the Spirit. He began to rejoice and to celebrate the goodness of a brand-new life.

Eleven years ago, I was led to teach a series in our Mid.Point services called *Finding Joy in the Journey*. The lessons took us on a journey of learning to live with joy regardless of circumstance. About halfway into the *Finding Joy in the Journey* series, our journey took a sharp turn. Our most trusted staff members begin to leave us in dramatic fashion. They influenced other members to leave. All in all, during the next few weeks Conroe Church saw the loss of about two-thirds of our membership. Within a few days of this, our unwed daughter was with child.

"How," I asked God, "am I supposed to teach *Finding Joy in the Journey* when I have lost my joy and my people?"

We are not allowed the choice of everything that happens in our lives. However, we are allowed to choose how we respond. In the next Mid.Point service, I moved to the next lesson and continued leading Conroe Church to *Finding Joy in the Journey.*

But it was different. The weeks before I had taught from a head filled with wisdom and man's learning. When we resumed the series, I taught with a heart that had no joy of its own but that understood the only source for my joy was Jesus Christ!

One week the Lord placed in my heart Psalm 34:1, and I led Conroe Church to celebrate the Lord "at all times." Good times, bad times, happy times, and broken times! God permitted that moment to come to us, and we could choose how to react in it. *I will bless the LORD at all times: his praise shall continually be in my mouth* (Psalm 34:1).

Another week our song of celebration was found in Psalm 89:1, and we sang in celebration of the mercies of the Lord. *I will sing of the mercies of the LORD for ever: with my mouth will I make known thy faithfulness to all generations.*

One Sunday I felt to celebrate the mercies of the Lord. "Church," I challenged, "let us think of the goodness of the Lord and celebrate that we have hope! Let us celebrate that we have an unending supply of the Lord's mercies that are minted and packaged for us every morning when we awake." *This I recall to my mind, therefore have I hope. It is of the LORD'S mercies that we are not consumed, because his compassions fail not. They are new every morning: great is thy faithfulness* (Lamentations 3:21-23).

On another occasion, I had looked around and seen that some other churches seemed to be doing much better than we, and the Lord led me to celebrate the wins and blessings of God that appeared to be in other churches. Conroe Church celebrated the kindness of Jesus to our fellow saints in other assemblies. *Rejoice with them that do rejoice, and weep with them that weep* (Romans 12:15).

I sought the Lord one week, and He directed me to Habakkuk's account of difficult seasons. That Wednesday we celebrated failed harvests, disappointing outcomes, and empty benches!

> *Although the fig tree shall not blossom, neither shall fruit be in the vines; the labour of the olive shall fail, and the fields shall yield no meat; the flock shall be cut off from the fold, and there shall be no herd in the stalls: yet I will rejoice in the LORD, I will joy in the God of my salvation* (Habakkuk 3:17-18).

That week I led the one-third remnant of Conroe Church to make the choice that regardless of what seemed a failed harvest, empty barns, and lost sheep, we would find joy in the God of our salvation. Conroe Church celebrated!

I led Conroe Church into a new culture of celebration. Every week we pause the service and share a win in someone's life, and Conroe Church celebrates.

Just two weeks ago we took a special offering. My son-in-law was led to give all his money. His little family did not fellowship with the other young families that day because Daddy gave all the money to Jesus. The next morning, he checked his bank account and was amazed to see an unexpected deposit for exactly ten times the amount of money he had given the day before. He called me excited and rejoicing. The next Sunday, the story was shared with Conroe Church, and the church celebrated!

The Discipline of Celebration

Learning the discipline of celebration moves beyond a behavior into a way of life. The world has a culture that celebrates nothing but themselves. But when one learns the art of celebrating others, celebrating the goodness of God, and celebrating the blessings of other people, he truly has learned the art of celebration.

The Discipline of Guidance

Guidance might be better understood in biblical language as being "led by the Spirit." "Follow the cloud" is a personal mantra that prompts my son, Trent, to laugh at me. His entire life I have used this term when I step off script in meeting or service.

Trent shakes his head and says, "Here we go again, following that cloud!"

While this has a tinge of humor and teasing on his part, I now am able to tease him in return. At times when he is leading Conroe Church, he pauses and says, "We are not sure what is next, but we will follow the cloud wherever God leads us."

The children of Israel escaped from Egypt and started their journey through the desert to the Promised Land. God had led them to and through the Red Sea. They followed Moses as Moses followed the guidance of God. In that season God chose to lead them by cloud in the daylight hours and a pillar of fire by night. *And the LORD went before them by day in a pillar of a cloud, to lead them the way; and by night in a pillar of fire, to give them light; to go by day and night* (Exodus 13:21).

When that cloud moved, Israel moved. When the cloud was still, Israel was still. Regardless of the time of day or night, when the cloud began to move, then Israel did so. Hence, my lifetime of endeavoring to follow this pattern personally and with Conroe Church.

For as many as are led by the Spirit of God, they are the sons of God (Romans 8:14). Paul wrote that the sons of God follow the leading of God. Accordingly, we find Paul led by God to Damascus, the desert of Syria, Jerusalem, a Macedonian call, three missionary journeys, a prison, Caesar's palace (the one in Rome, not Las Vegas), and eventually an untimely death, after which his body was hidden and forgotten in the catacombs beneath Rome.

His birth and his death mattered little to him. What mattered was his journey. We celebrate a life sold out and led by the Spirit of God. *The Message* transliteration presents this verse thus: *God's Spirit beckons. There are things to do and places to go!*

God's Spirit beckons! He beckoned Abram from Ur. He beckoned Moses and Israel from Egypt. He beckoned three disciples into a revelation of transfiguration on the mountainside. God beckoned Peter to step from the security of his safe reality on his boat to walk on the very unstable reality of water beside Himself.

Jesus Christ the same yesterday, and to day, and for ever (Hebrews 13:8). Nothing about God has changed! He led in biblical times, He leads today, and He will lead tomorrow. He led my grandfathers and father. He now leads me and my children. He will lead my grandchildren and great-grandchildren. His nature and promises are unchanging.

Peter's message at Pentecost included this affirmation of God's intent to lead and fill us with His present power and guidance moving forward, regardless of geographical or generational location. *For the promise is unto you, and to your children, and to all that are afar off, even as many as the Lord our God shall call* (Acts 2:39).

Maintaining a Spirit-led life, though, must also be a Scripture-led life. We must gain understanding of the Word of God and embrace with certainty that God's leading will never violate His Word.

I once knew of a minister who divorced his wife and married a much younger, prettier one. When asked about this, he answered, "God told me to divorce my first wife and to marry this one."

The response of everyone who hears such should be a simple, guttural, "Huh?"

A member once said, "God has led me not to tithe."

My fleshly response would have been, "You are the first one; let me know how things work out." But my Spirit-led response was simply, "Let's pray about this together." Soon the member wandered into other spiritual delusions.

The Word of God speaks clearly in matters of tithing, divorce, and a plethora of other principles. God never overrides His Word with a personal or verbal word more convenient for our personal desires.

God also places pastors and other elders in our lives for the sake of counsel concerning life decisions. Too often we seek personal affirmation rather than the guidance of good leadership and the direction of God.

The young man came by the office for "counsel." He asked if he should buy a new pick-up truck. As a pastor I try to avoid being party to such decisions, so instead of replying, I posed questions. "Do you need a truck? Can you afford a new truck? Does your wife know about this new truck?"

Finally, he sheepishly responded, "Well, Pastor, I already bought the truck, and it is out in the parking lot. I just wanted to bring it by to show it to you!"

Earlier I shared how God led us in planting Conroe Church through prayer and fasting. God leads, never varying from His established principles. Many of the disciplines discussed in this writing work together in the processes of our being led by God.

I have led Conroe Church for thirty-one years. Daily I seek His voice and guidance. I have lived with a simple principle I find in Psalm 127:1. Consistently, I have sought Him, and He has led me. I accept that this is God's church, and He accomplishes His will. I am only an under-shepherd to the Great Shepherd. *Except the LORD build the house, they labour in vain that build it* (Psalm 127:1).

Conroe Church was in yet another transitional moment. I had done all I knew to do to move forward with an issue. I had prayed, fasted, gathered our board, sought godly counsel from elders, and asked my father's advice, but still I felt helpless. I had no further options. The arm of the flesh did not have the strength or wisdom for this occasion. I besought the Lord, and He sent a dream.

In the dream, I was frantically searching for answers within Conroe Church. I hurried from the sanctuary to the lobby to the classrooms and across the street to Conroe Christian School. Nowhere did I find the answer.

Then amid my dream the Lord took me to the corner of my office and said, "Tear out the sheetrock."

I removed the drywall and found a door; He led me to open and enter it. Behind that door I found offices and classrooms fully furnished and waiting to be utilized. I marveled, for it seemed I had known of these hidden rooms all the time. I recalled building them and then covering the door. In reality I knew I had not, but the dream was quite real.

Then God spoke, "Just as I have shown you hidden resources already in place for you, I have placed within Conroe Church everything that you need to accomplish My plans. Stop worrying!"

In an instant, all anxiety for the future of the church subsided, and I continue to marvel when I see God reveal yet another "room" or talent or ministry. My faith remains affirmed and unwavering in the future of this ministry.

This work began as a discussion of the hand of God in my personal spiritual formation. It has grown far beyond a written narrative into a living documentary of my journey. Now, I share one more example of the discipline of guidance in my life that happened only this week.

The initial draft of this project required less than three weeks. I prayerfully approached each discipline and asked for the right words of wisdom to make this a document of inspiration for those who encounter it. Needless to say, my days have been filled with writing, reading, and listening for the still, small whisper of what God would have me to pen.

Two days ago, I paused, went into the sanctuary of Conroe Church, and settled into "my spot." I asked God to speak into my spirit the perfect words to share with you. I strained to hear His response. I stretched my ears as far as I could. I was asking God to guide me, to lead me. For two days I wrote nothing even though I felt the pressure of my deadlines. Throughout those two days, I meditated and lived within the silence of God.

Then He began to speak. He began to lead me in that familiar way He has led and guided me for my lifetime. He spoke to me concerning this section and gave clear direction concerning the upcoming discussion of worship.

I believe that God leads and guides us into all truth and principle. He leads us into His truths, which always are confirmed by the principles of the Word of God. *Howbeit when he, the Spirit of truth, is come, he will guide you into all truth: for he shall not speak of himself; but whatsoever he shall hear, that shall he speak: and he will shew you things to come* (John 16:13).

Formation of a Worshiper

Every author of disciplines I read includes in his list the discipline of worship. I have purposely not connected this discipline to any list of disciplines, for I feel worship is the essence of every spiritual discipline. The core of spiritual formation is wrapped completely in our worship.

The Pauline Epistles often employ the term "conversation," which might be better defined as "manner of living." I consider worship a "conversation" or "manner of living." Worship is a way of life!

From the beginning, God formed man with the power of choice. His greatest desire is that each of us will be a worshiper. The first recorded human-to-human conflict occurred between two brothers who chose to worship differently.

The showdown on Mount Carmel between Elijah and the prophets of Baal instructed Israel that it matters whom, how, what, and when one worships. Each of us possesses the innate propensity to worship. Israel had drifted from proper worship into the worship of false idols.

Jesus spoke to this concept to His disciples.

But the hour cometh, and now is, when the true worshippers shall worship the Father in spirit and in truth: for the Father seeketh such to worship him. God is a Spirit: and they that worship him must worship him in spirit and in truth (John 4:23-24).

One cannot be a worshiper without acknowledging the Spirit of God. Likewise, every worshiper must pursue the disciplines of walking with Christ. Jesus defined such worship as "true worship." True worship is more than a song list and haze machine on Sunday morning. Worship encompasses the very being and nature of the true worshiper. Our determination to worship will greatly influence our decisions, lifestyle, entertainments, integrity, and simply every aspect of life.

As with all other disciplines, worship is not a destination but rather a journey, manner of living, conversation, choice, and lifestyle. Worship comprises the heart of all spiritual discipline.

This accounting of my spiritual formation originally fulfilled an assignment from a professor and my mentor team. I wrote knowing they would read and evaluate if I have successfully navigated the process. They have the right and obligation to assess me and to make judgments. I understand that other men will make decisions about me as well, based on what they read here.

The words of the apostle Peter echo in my mind when I consider the preceding paragraph. *Then Peter and the other apostles answered and said, We ought to obey God rather than men* (Acts 5:29).

Men will read this. They will form opinions of the accounting of my journey. As you read this in book format, you have made and will make judgments of me based upon this accounting. I am being assessed by you. What an honor!

However, the greatest assessment will come from the great Assessor. This study reaffirms in my heart the mandate to prove mastery in these disciplines that pleases God. For while man might read this and approve or disapprove, what God assesses in my life and heart is eternal.

News alert! He assesses yours as well! For the essence of the spiritual disciplines is worship, and the essence of worship is spiritual discipline.

The discussion of faith versus works has gone long. One group insists that an orphanage in a third-world country signifies mature formation. Another declares that no number of orphanages anywhere in the world merits God's grace.

Abraham fully intended to offer Isaac as an act of faith and trust in the Almighty. This was no mere empty confession but rather a principle in action. Likewise, Rahab put everything on the line when she hid the Israelite spies. Works and faith are inseparable. Just as rays cannot be separated from the sun, neither can faith and works be separated.

> *I can already hear one of you agreeing by saying, "Sounds good. You take care of the faith department, I'll handle the works department." Not so fast. You can no more show me your works apart from your faith than I can show you my faith apart from my works. Faith and works, works and faith, fit together hand in glove* (James 2:18, MSG).

As an Apostolic Pentecostal preacher, I practice and lead others to pursue certain disciplines. These disciplines are not salvific in themselves. My pursuit of the Master prompts me to practice certain disciplines so that I might better know Him. My old preacher daddy often says, "You don't get good to get God, but you get God to get good."

The practice or pursuit of any discipline then is not representative of any legal or theological demand. I have never seen a checklist handed to the new convert before he leaves the altar that mandates all the things he must do now to "stay" saved. However, I have seen thousands of newly minted children of God experience the new birth and immediately begin both discarding and acquiring things in their personal lives they feel might serve as either a hindrance or an asset respectively in their new pursuit of their relationship with the Lord.

My wife and I were in a local department store when we happened upon a new convert. She greeted us with hugs and appreciation. She began to explain to us that she needed some new clothes because what she had always worn was not conducive to her new life.

Some will say such an action is completely unnecessary or even legalistic. But for this new baby in Christ, these actions were the pursuit of a new discipline of pleasing her Lord. She unknowingly but instantly acted upon the spiritual truth that she was now a worshiper, and as a new worshiper, she must act and live in a manner pleasing to the One she had chosen to worship.

This new worshiper had unwittingly stumbled upon the reality of worship: a culture of disciplines that enhance the worship experience. Paul wrote of this to the struggling saints at Corinth. *What? know ye not that your body is the temple of the Holy Ghost which is in you, which ye have of God, and ye are not your own?* (1 Corinthians 6:19).

Our dear young convert was growing to understand that she had become a dwelling place of the Holy Ghost. She could not yet have understood the theology or doctrines of grace, but she knew she was no longer in control of her own life. She understood she now belonged to God. This new knowledge would expand within her as she matured, but in that moment, her worship was displayed as a need to bring certain disciplines into her life so she might be pleasing to the One whom she worshiped.

Without a New Beginnings class or catechism of church rules, she knew not only that her life had new owner-ship but also that her life had been changed. Somebody or something had paid a significant price for the joy she now had. Paul also wrote of this to the Corinthians. *For ye are bought with a price: therefore glorify God in your body, and in your spirit, which are God's* (1 Corinthians 6:20).

Instinctively, this young woman began to react to the work of grace in her life. No teaching was required for her to act upon this development in her life. God was already at work in her. He was forming a new creature in Christ. Liter-ally, we were observing the transformation as old things were removed and new things added in her. Day by day, one thing at a time, she changed. Her alteration was both internal and external, for the work of grace manifested in her. She was becoming one of those living epistles Paul wrote of. *Ye are our epistle written in our hearts, known and read of all men* (2 Corinthians 3:2). A worshiper is on a journey of re-acting to the work of God within his life by embracing new disciplines willingly and joyfully.

Rammie visited Conroe Church on Easter Sunday 2021. He was a nice, cowboy-looking guy with a huge grin. I introduced myself, and he responded, "I know who you are! I have been watching you online every Sunday for six months. You always say to the online viewers, 'If you think the service is good there in your house, you should come and experience how good it is at our house!' Pastor, I have come to see how good it is here!"

He has not missed a service. He went to a conference with our men, and God filled him with the Holy Ghost. Soon he was baptized in Jesus' name. He purchased a big, three-hundred-dollar, designer Bible. Then he bought a hand-tooled leather Bible cover. He joined a small group that studies discipleship. He started cooking and feeding the group. He formed relationships with the group members and helps them all. He joined the First Impressions team. He personally makes sure the restrooms stay fresh so our guests are not inconvenienced. He asks me weekly if there are any tasks I might need help with. Today, he has taken a church vehicle for an oil change and cleaning and even purchased new registration. Last week during a prayer service he noticed an area needed vacuuming and took care of it.

Rammie is worshiping via his new fellowship and service, but to him he is showing gratitude for the great work of the Spirit in his life. Unbeknownst to himself, new disciplines are forming as he continues to worship the Lord!

Such is the process of the formation of a worshiper. This is not just true for new believers. Mature and seasoned saints of God too continue to be formed into worshipers. The formation is not instantaneous. Formation requires time and submission. Formation requires all the spiritual disciplines. And while the good saint of God may have been a church member for many years, God is never quite finished with us.

Mike is one of the seasoned saints who allows formation to continue in him. After his fourth retirement as a communications engineer, he and his wife joined a small Bible study group that utilizes video for instruction. Mike sits on the board of Conroe Church and has been a faithful member for many years, but he took a bold new step. He became the "technology officer" of the Bible study group. He keeps the equipment running. He comes by the office and "needs" some help. We stop and help him. He recruits others in his journey of making sure there is adequate technological coverage for the next meeting.

Mike is experiencing continued formation. His entire life he has been faithful to attend church. His giving has been like clockwork. He was faithful to God in every way. He literally would mail his tithe back to the church when he traveled or worked out of town. I would tease him about "mailing in" his relationship with God. In this new venture, Mike felt the weight of responsibility for making sure the video equipment was fully operational. He is discovering a new way to worship by serving his small group.

Formation is a process of constant reformation. The formation of our worship is constantly in motion. We never quite arrive. This constant pursuit is a two-way street. God continues to form us as we continue to seek Him. Or do we continue to seek Him so He will continue to form us? Regardless of what happens first, such formation always results in newness. *Behold, I will do a new thing; now it shall spring forth; shall ye not know it? I will even make a way in the wilderness, and rivers in the desert* (Isaiah 43:19).

I grow excited when I observe these new things in the lives of Conroe Church members. One of our men started a small group for guitar players. Ironically, he did not play the guitar. He bought himself a nice acoustic guitar, and the group would meet weekly. A few weeks later I looked up and saw this great man playing his guitar during the Sunday morning service; I rejoiced at this new thing. Last Sunday I was even more excited to see that his thirteen-year-old son was also on the stage, playing his new guitar. Father and son both experienced a new thing as they worshiped by guitar!

What new thing is God doing within you? What new discipline of worship is growing inside you? What new consecration is developing in your mind or spirit? What dream is stirring you? Allow this thing to unfold! Do not be afraid!

Last evening in our youth and young adult service, a visiting Bible-school student timidly prayed for a man. I halted his prayer and told him to lay his hand confidently on the young man and to pray boldly. I added, "Pray louder than the voice of intimidation you hear while praying."

After the service the young student came and thanked me for the instruction. "I know God is calling me to be a more effective altar worker. You helped me tonight!"

New things require new disciplines. These new disciplines are all encompassed in our worship. Worshipers are born, then formed again and again.

A new member recently shared with me his desire to attend church and simply worship. I happily agreed to this but explained such a commitment. "You are welcome to come to worship. Everyone needs a place to come face to face with God and simply worship." I then encouraged the individual to worship as much as he wanted but to be prepared for what would happen.

I explained, "Worship will create a greater desire to worship. That greater desire to worship will grow and begin to manifest in a desire to serve."

He said, "But I do not want to serve. I want to heal."

"That is wonderful, but your worship is progressive and formative. Your worship will result instinctively in a fresh desire to serve."

"Let's see."

"Yes, let's do, but be careful!"

"Why?" he inquired.

"Your worship will create a new desire to serve. Then as you serve, a new desire to lead will be birthed."

"I don't think so."

"Yes, we will, but meanwhile consider where you would like to serve and lead."

I continue to watch as this progression of worship forms new disciplines in the new church member, for the discipline of worship creates a desire to draw closer to God. As we draw closer to Him, He draws closer to us. When we are close to Him, we grow in desire to serve and to be more like Him.

I knew a man who had great talent with ministry to children. His public job informed him of a transfer. He told his company he appreciated the job and offer but wished to decline. When asked why, he told them, "This company is my job, but my children's ministry work at my church is my calling. I only need this job to support my calling. If the job goes away, I will just get another job!"

His ministry to children was the way he worshiped.

Worship, the Essence
of Spiritual Disciplines

Superimpose any of the spiritual disciplines over worship, and you will continue to see them both distinctly. They are distinct, but they are the same. The very essence of these disciplines is the essence of worship.

Consider the discipline of meditation. We call the desire to hear the voice of God in quietness and to commune with Him meditation. Time spent in meditation results in a greater desire to be a worshiper. Meditation adds to the formation of worship in us. We meditate because we worship, and we worship because we meditate.

The discipline of prayer is similar in that the practice of prayer generates the desire to pray more. A healthy and developed prayer life manifests itself in this strong pull to worship. Or does our desire to worship the Lord and to draw closer to Him ignite our motivation to pray more? The pursuit of prayer is really a desire to worship, and the more we worship, the closer at hand prayer stands.

Likewise, the discipline of fasting blends into our worship. Our worship kindles the desire to deny our fleshly hungers, so we say, "No," to our desires in fasting. As our fasting distances us from our flesh and worldly desires, our worship becomes more animated and pure. When the church fasts together, the next few worship services are amazing. Our pure worship compels us to pursue fasting just as fasting propels our worship to greater dimensions.

As a matter of course, the hunger for the discipline of study emerges the more we worship. We worship and draw closer to God. We desire to know Him. That desire creates more desire for truth. Therefore, we spend time in the Word of God. Time spent in study of the Word enhances our love for truth. Truth then produces a greater desire for true worship. Worship and truth mandate developing habits of study. We study and learn and hide the Word of God in our hearts. Our love for truth and study prompts pure worship. Truly, we learn that pursuit of the Word and things of God births the worship of a true worshiper since our worship is of the spirit and our study is of the Word. They are inseparable!

Balance the discipline of simplicity with worship. Neither tips the scale above the other. Pure, simple worship results in pure, simple living. The practice of moderation helps declutter our lives of things that distract us. The removal of those distractions allows a greater freedom in our worship. Maybe worship removes the need for more material things, or maybe setting aside those same material things allows us a greater freedom in our worship. Regardless, the two are fused.

The silence of solitude reverberates over the soul of the worshiper. I ask myself, *Am I reveling alone and silent in the presence of God, or am I worshiping?* The worshiper learns to be content in the crowd or when isolated, for both are alone time with the only One who really matters. Alone time with God is worship time with Him, just as worship time in a multitude is also alone time with God!

Pursuing the discipline of submission also is marked by worship. We worship the Object of our submission. We worship the One we submit to. My submission is a wellspring of my worship, while my worship is effortless since I have chosen submission. I clap my hands in submission in the same way I tithe in worship. As worship superimposes submission, I cannot tell where my submission begins and my worship ends.

The discipline of service stands tall, for it removes the daunting question, "What is in it for me?" Worship does the same. The worshiper designates his worship for God as he does his service to the kingdom. He serves because he worships, and he worships because he serves. Because worshipers love to worship, the discipline is not an effort. Worship includes serving. Service is no more sacrifice than worship. To take service from a worshiper or worship from a servant strips him of his greatest significance.

One should approach the discipline of confession with joy as confession removes all inhibitions from worship. He confesses to a trusted brother. Likewise, when a brother trusts him in confession, they both rejoice. Confessors confess to confessors, and both either accept or forgive the other. Such confession is an act of worship. The confessor does not want his sin to come between himself and God. Neither does the other want to withhold forgiveness from his brother for the same reason. Confession aids one's worship, and worship encourages his confession. Therefore, when the minister opens the altar, the confessor wants to be first there while his brother is just behind, helping him with forgiveness and brotherly love. Worshiping alone is wonderful, but when one worships with the brother who has confessed or has forgiven, the experience is beyond wonderful.

When the discipline of celebration is practiced, joy is evidenced every day. The celebrant walks in joy. He goes about his day in joy. He suffers in joy. He gives with joy rather than regret. Worship is just like joy. The celebrant chooses to worship and finds joy in everything he does. He cannot separate his joy from his worship. His worship is liberated by joy, and his joy is liberated by his worship.

After pursuing the discipline of guidance, one comes to understand that being led by the Holy Spirit and worshiping the Almighty are inseparable. A worshiper seeks God's leading while His leading leads to worship. Worship incites the need for godly guidance. Like each of the disciplines, it is impossible to practice His guidance and fail to worship.

Since you have made it this far with me, thank you! Let me simply say again that worship is the essence of all the spiritual disciplines, and the disciplines are the very essence of the worship. To echo James's lesson on works and faith, I will show you my disciplines by my worship and my worship by my disciplines.

Penning the account of my spiritual journey clarifies a reality that I have lived but now better understand how to articulate. Everything thing I do, every discipline I embrace, every choice I make, every decision I consider is to be done with the reality that I am a worshiper. Therefore, every action of my life must be done in a manner that reflects my adoration of my Lord.

My schedule for today must be planned with the priority that it belongs to God and I am but a steward of this collection of 1,140 minutes. *This is the day which the LORD hath made; we will rejoice and be glad in it* (Psalm 118:24).

This familiar verse declares truth that daily I must embrace. The Lord made this day. It belongs to Him. What I do with this gift is completely my priority. It also gives me guidance as to what I am to do with this collection of minutes. I am to rejoice (worship) and be glad!

The clarion purpose of this day is to worship. I am handed a gift of 1,140 minutes that God designed to be filled with worship that will give glory to Him. Couple this with the truth found in 1 Corinthians. *What? know ye not that your body is the temple of the Holy Ghost?* (1 Corinthians 6:19). I am the dwelling place of the Spirit of God. I am His temple. I have been filled with the Holy Ghost. A temple is a place of worship. I am a place of worship. My body is a place of worship.

The apostle John was exiled on the island called Patmos when he penned his incredible revelation. In his greeting he spoke of tribulation and patience. He acknowledged his reality of exile. Those in his day understood that John was in the Alcatraz of his day, exiled and forgotten by man but not by God!

In this moment of undesired circumstance, he heard the voice of God. God speaks even when we are lost, forgotten, exiled, and left to die. God still speaks. John in that moment was a living example that even a day in an ugly place like Patmos is created by God.

The same God who had created the day David killed Goliath awakened John on Patmos. We are given examples that whether we use our day to kill an uncircumcised giant or we spend that same time waking up in a God-forsaken reality of exile and doom, the day remains the Lord's.

God's allotment of days to John included the one when he awoke on Patmos and heard that incredible voice of God. John understood that even on Patmos the day is the Lord's. He knew it might well be his last day. Regardless of every rational drawback, John's morning on Patmos was also God's. God spoke, and John wrote. *I was in the Spirit on the Lord's day* (Revelation 1:10).

If David encouraged himself in worship, Paul and Silas worshiped in prison, and John was worshiping in exile, I have no excuse for not being a worshiper. My day is the Lord's day. I am mandated to offer rejoicing and joy.

Every single thing I fill this day with must be premeditated for worship. This living temple must echo the high praise of its steward to its Creator. Therefore, I must carefully consider the things I pack into this day!

I determine these things by passing every aspect of my day through 1 Corinthians 6:20. *Therefore glorify God in your body, and in your spirit, which are God's* (1 Corinthians 6:20). The next two chapters will reflect how I filter my agenda and experiences daily through this verse. I will also share how I, as a pastor, shepherd the Conroe Church family into becoming worshipers in their daily lives.

Glorify God in Your Body

The lifestyle of the Apostolic Pentecostal is designed by God to give glory to Himself. *Therefore glorify God in your body* (1 Corinthians 6:20). Thus, as a new Christian matures, his desire to grow closer to his Redeemer increases the desire to distance himself from the old life.

When I was seventeen years old, our family was invited for a cookout at the home of a church family. This nice family had a pool table in their garage. Having never been around a pool table, I was doing a stellar job of acting like I was a pool shark when Dad walked in. He looked at me and said, "Kent, I didn't realize you played pool." He said this with that dad inflection of rebuke and inquisition.

I missed another shot and looked at my father, recognizing I had crossed some unspoken line. I said, "Neither did I, Dad," and returned the pool stick to the rack. That was the grand finale of my career as a pool shark.

This is not a commentary on whether the game of pool is right or wrong. In all reality, the game itself is innocent. But to my old preacher daddy, who had been a pool gambler in his young adult years, the game of pool was something he had set aside in consecration to God. This activity represented the old creature. In consequence, Dad no longer played pool, and as I learned that day, he preferred his oldest son not do so either.

That day was lesson day for me. Dad taught me that some things are consecrated to God. Dad had consecrated his life of pool and gambling to God. He could play pool if he desired to; the game was not a sin. But to him, he set the game aside in his life because his desire to worship the Lord was greater than his desire for the game.

We all recognize the "thou shalt nots" in the Word of God. That day I learned the principle that all things are not a "thou shalt not"; rather, some things are "I choose not" for the sake of my walk with God. This life lesson journeys with me more than forty years later.

Standing by a pool table in a hot garage in Aransas Pass, Texas, I discovered the filter of 1 Corinthians 6:20. My spiritual journey has included the daily application of a filter that asks this simple question: "Does this glorify God?"

My life is not my own. I was purchased by God. The name of Jesus appears on the warranty deed of the Temple of God located at the intersection of Kent Smith and Life. Every activity at this temple must glorify God. Hence, I intentionally "glorify God in [my] body"!

Let me share with you the practical applications I use to glorify God in my body. My hygiene goes through this filter. Daily I arise and attempt to exercise in some manner. I often go to the gym to spend time with the friendly elliptical machine. I walk around the block with our puppy. While I realize that "bodily exercise profiteth little," I also know I must guard and maintain this temple God gave me. I strive in some way to maintain my body for the Lord.

I look at myself in the mirror and survey me. I assess whether I need a haircut. I shave daily. I want my temple to be acceptable for any who choose to visit with me today.

The custom of Pentecost asks our men to have clean haircuts. The Bible briefly speaks to the fact of the shame if a man has long hair. This has traditionally been interpreted men should wear their hair cut over the ears and clear of the collar. However, this interpretation is not a law of God. Instead, it is an effort to provide a working guideline. But the bottom line is this: I keep my hair the way I do, not for the sake of a rule or scriptural mandate. I keep my hair as I do for the sake of my worship. If I am to glorify God in my body, I am worshiping when I follow a scriptural principle for not wearing "long hair," but the greater principle I practice is that this forms part of the way I worship.

I lead Conroe Church similarly. Seldom do I publicly teach on this subject, but I example it and ask our staff to example it. On a few occasions I have sidled up to a young man and asked if he needs me to help him get a haircut, and we all laugh. This is not the enforcing of a rule but the impartation of a principle to "glorify God."

Likewise, I wear my face clean shaven. Daily, I go to the trouble of shaving off the stubble. The Bible is basically silent about facial hair. It does not say, "Thou shalt not wear a whisker!" However, the custom of Pentecost developed over the last several years for men to be clean shaven, not for the sake of a rule but for the sake of our worship. My daily shaving is my submission to the worship of my Lord.

My manner of dress is that of moderation. Paul taught that we should be moderate and modest in all things. Thus, I endeavor to dress appropriately for any occasion, maintaining modesty and moderation as part of my worship.

I do not wear sleeveless shirts or short pants for this reason. I try to wear sleeves to my elbows. Likewise, I do not wear short pants and endeavor to lead the men of Conroe Church to do the same. I often share, "Gentlemen, nobody wants to look up your sleeve and see your armpit; neither do they want to look up your short pants leg as you sit sprawled out." While no declaration says, "Short pants are a sin!" I endeavor to lead our men to forgo shorts and tank-type shirts as a part of their glorifying God in their bodies.

In today's culture we are seeing an increase in tattoos. I marvel when men or women come to God and instinctively begin to cover their body art. There is no reason for a church or pastor to shame anyone who comes to God with such tattooing. Those markings were acquired before the Lord was given lordship of their lives. Thus, there should never be any hint of shame from the pulpit or the pew. At the same time, I encourage our members to forgo such body marking. Such body marking is indicative of an old way of life and an old manner of worship. But to show our worship now as new, blood-bought creatures in Christ, we should not mark or tattoo our bodies.

Here is a neat little secret about body art and Jesus. When we come to Christ all things are made new. The old man becomes a new man. Our sins are washed away in baptism. Those sins are removed from us. Not even God can remember what those sins were. Likewise, if God cannot see our sins, I have confidence neither can He see that tattoo of a naked woman on your arm, sir! Saints might see it. The church might see it, and even the preacher might see it. On the contrary, God cannot!

I do not drink any alcoholic beverage due to a commitment to my Lord and an expression of worship. Regularly Tracie and I have a waiter approach our table and remove the wine menu, saying emphatically, "You will not need this." The evidence of active worship speaks loudly.

I am careful with my hobbies and entertainments. The way I entertain myself indicates my values in life. I lead Conroe Church to choose their entertainments carefully. The 1 Corinthians 6:20 filter should be applied to every pastime. Does this amusement give glory to God? Some things do not necessarily give glory and really are not a question for us. The application of the filter should be, "Does this activity have the potential to give glory to anything or anyone beside the Lord?"

I attend church each time the doors are open. I lead Conroe Church accordingly. I taught my family that nothing is more important than church attendance. I hope to example the priority of faithfulness. My church attendance is not a mandated rule; rather, I choose to attend faithfully as part of my worship.

I glorify God with my body in the places I go and also in the places I choose not to go. I often teach Conroe Church that once they have taken up their crosses and are following Jesus, the "crosses" will prevent their entrance through some doors. "If one must lay down his cross to pass through some door of opportunity or entertainment, then that opportunity is not of God," I explain.

The lifestyle choices I make as a man and a pastor are intentional. I am mandated to moderate my lifestyle for the singular purpose of glorifying God in my body. Such choices are part of my daily worship.

Just as I make lifestyle choices that are examples for those I lead, so does my wife. Tracie has been an excellent example of lifestyle choices for the ladies of Conroe Church.

Pentecostal ladies are known for their long hair and dresses. Often, they have felt the criticism of those who do not understand their lifestyle choices, but these wonderful ladies understand the scriptural teaching of modesty and proper attire. The principle of ladies' not wearing what would appear to signify a man, or man's apparel, is clear in Scripture. Therefore, our Pentecostal ladies are careful not to wear trousers. Instead, they wear skirts or dresses.

This is a lifestyle decision that is not based upon rules, for when our ladies dress for the day, they choose to wear apparel that pleases the Lord. They do not condemn others who might not practice such. However, they model a practiced discipline of their worship of the Lord.

Pentecostal ladies worship through their modesty by not exposing too much of their erogenous areas. They wear knee-length skirting and moderate venting or slits along with moderately sleeved blouses, making sure the necks of their blouses are modest. This is not an effort of control over the ladies, nor is this an attempt to make them frumpy or unattractive. Instead, these practices of modesty and moderation are significant of their worship to the Lord.

We once had a beautiful young lady receive the gift of the Holy Ghost. Her dress that morning indicated her career choice of a bar dancer. To say the least, her dress was too short on both ends! As her rejoicing subsided, she began to pull at the neck of the dress to cover herself, but when she pulled the dress neck up, the hem rose, too. Literally, she was pulling up on one end of the dress and down on the other. In an instant, she felt the transforming power of the Lord. Instinctively, she felt the need to embrace disciplines of modesty, for now she was a worshiper!

Pentecostal ladies practice the discipline of not cutting their hair. While the New Testament teaches clearly on this subject, our ladies do not practice this discipline as a rule but as another discipline such as fasting or prayer. These disciplines are how they worship.

Likewise, our ladies do not wear cosmetics that change the natural color of their complexions. Some ladies might wear a bit of some sort of coverup for a blemish's sake, but overall, Pentecostal ladies understand they are fearfully and wonderfully created by God. Their natural beauty gives glory to God. Overuse of cosmetic shifts focus from godly beauty to fleshly beauty. Pentecostal ladies gladly embrace this self-discipline, demonstrating Paul's recommendation to "glorify God in [their] body."

It is commonly understood that morality and marital fidelity are defined in the Scriptures. It can be quite simple for this to become legalistic; however, such things are better addressed as being part of our worship. I am faithful to my marriage vows not because the Bible insists or even because I love Tracie. I am faithful to the vows I have made before the Lord as evidence of my worship. Oh, yes, I worship Tracie, but I worship the Lord more!

When Vice-president Pence was highly criticized for not riding alone in a vehicle with a female reporter, he cited that he had made a covenant not to spend time alone with any lady other than Mrs. Pence. This is an honorable if sometimes inconvenient commitment. I have made a similar commitment. Neither do I have casual telephone visits, text messaging, or online communities for the same reasons. My purpose is twofold. First, I love Tracie and never want to do anything to jeopardize her trust. But the greatest reason is because I love the Lord. This commitment is representative of another way I choose to offer worship to Him.

Biblical principles of personal integrity are matters I have come to observe. Many passages of Scripture address this. Paul instructed Timothy to live with honor, a great recommendation for each of us. However, I choose to live with honor and integrity as a part of my worship to the Lord. Yes, I pay my bills because I owe them; however, I pay my bills because I worship the Lord. I am faithful to my wife because I worship Him. Literally, everything I do passes through my 1 Corinthians 6:20 filter.

These few things and a myriad more are simply examples of the formative process of God working on me and showing me how to lead our people. Though not necessarily spiritual, they have a great impact on spiritual outcomes. These are ways we have chosen to honor the Lord in worship by embracing 1 Corinthians 6:20 and giving God glory with our physical bodies.

Glorify God in Your Spirit

lorify God . . . in your spirit (1 Corinthians 6:20). Spiritual growth is a journey. In the previous chapter I addressed the practice of certain personal disciplines and behaviors for the sake of giving God glory with our bodies. Such physical practices provide a very measurable outcome.

Some may well judge themselves or others by the outward display of disciplines, especially when some might consider the outward manifestations or lack thereof significant in a comparative sense. Jesus handled this tendency in a parable.

The Lord indicated that He stood near the Pharisee and listened to him pray, "Lord, I am so grateful I am not like this publican!" This account stands as a stellar example of the failure of comparative discipline. While the Pharisee considered himself better than the publican, the Lord expressed his preference for the attitude of the penitent publican over the pride of the Pharisee.

Pride is just one example of the inward failure that so easily happens within each of us. When we are mandated to glorify God in our spirits but manifest pride over another, we exhibit the false elevation of ourselves over another.

We must not gauge the quality of our worship or disciplines by outward manifestations. A Pentecostal lady might always wear a dress and her husband never get caught being a pool shark as I did, but that does not automatically make them worshipers.

153

Carl came into my life in Oklahoma City in 1980. He was freshly appointed as a missionary, and he radiated the joy of his new calling. Shortly thereafter, his wife died with cancer, and his missionary appointment was rescinded. He lost his wife and his ministry appointment at the same time. He had young children at home, no job, and a broken heart. He found himself in the middle of bankruptcy. He never quite found his way back into a fulfilling ministry.

Carl later would marry Shirley, and they lived next door to us for the last twenty-five years of his life. Upon his passing last year, I pondered my observations of him. He had lost everything. His calling had been pulled from beneath his feet. Some years later he was betrayed by men he trusted with his life and future. He seemed to be a modern-day Job.

This man became my modern-day, living epistle of 1 Corinthians 6:20, for daily he modeled how to "glorify God in [his] spirit." He was my friend for forty-plus years. He was my father-in-law for thirty-five years and my next-door neighbor for twenty-five years. Never did I hear a complaint or criticism of any circumstance life presented him.

Shortly before he passed away, he gave me a letter with his desires for his memorial service. His instructions included his desire for select ministers to say a few words. I was amazed and dismayed to see, listed among those he had invited to speak at his funeral, some of the men who had betrayed him the most severely! Even in death, Carl modeled to his family how to glorify God in one's spirit.

We must glorify God in our spirits. We must allow the work of the Holy Ghost to be so alive within us that the outward manifestations of our worship and lifestyle choices reveal the inner man.

This morning I shared some of this project with my niece. She replied, "Uncle Kent, the outside stuff is easy. It's all the inside stuff that is a challenge." She got it! We must glorify God in our spirits.

I am a late baby boomer. My generation was quite well versed in qualifying the saints by assessing the outward display of disciplines rather than insisting that an inward practice of holiness was much more important than any legalized standard. Standards are important, but having a right heart and spirit is more important.

When I glorify God in my spirit, I display the fruit of the Spirit. *But the fruit of the Spirit is love, joy, peace, longsuffering, gentleness, goodness, faith, meekness, temperance: against such there is no law* (Galatians 5:22-23).

A few days ago while teaching, my son, Trent, encouraged the saints to be happy and joyful in their walks with God. "Be one of those people who have that happy Holy Ghost, not one who got the mean Holy Ghost!" Funny, but true. To worship God in our spirits we must exhibit the happy Holy Ghost, not the mean one!

The Conclusion of Spiritual Formation

Spiritual formation is a constant process. God works in us, and we pursue Him by embracing disciplines. This two-way process is capsulated herein: *Draw nigh to God, and he will draw nigh to you. Cleanse your hands, ye sinners; and purify your hearts, ye double minded* (James 4:8).

In this single verse we find the completeness of spiritual formation, spiritual disciplines, and worship.

1. God forms and fills us with His Spirit.
2. We endeavor to draw nigh to God via the practice of spiritual disciplines.
3. As we move closer to Him, He moves closer to us.
4. We "glorify God in [our bodies]" by making sure we have "clean hands" (Psalm 24:4).
5. We "glorify God in . . . [our spirits]" by ensuring the purity of our hearts.

How does one conclude the concept of spiritual formation? I think it near impossible to do so in this life, for our formation is not a destination but a journey. We never quite get there until we reach heaven. Our arrival at successful spiritual formation is not accomplished in this life but is pursued in this life and accomplished in the next one.

The great king Solomon came to the end of his journey in Ecclesiastes when he penned these valuable words:

Let us hear the conclusion of the whole matter: Fear God, and keep his commandments: for this is the whole duty of man (Ecclesiastes 12:13).

The Amplified translation conveys this summary better than any other.

> *All has been heard; the end of the matter is: Fear God [revere and worship Him, knowing that He is] and keep His commandments, for this is the whole of man [the full, original purpose of his creation, the object of God's providence, the root of character, the foundation of all happiness, the adjustment to all inharmonious circumstances and conditions under the sun] and the whole [duty] for every man* (Ecclesiastes 12:13, AMP).

This project began as a paper and ended an epistle—if not to you, then absolutely to me. I have revisited my spiritual beginnings and shared examples of those lessons God has bequeathed to me. My spiritual formation continues, even after fifty-three years of being filled with the Holy Ghost and preaching to others for forty-six years. Paul said it best as I quoted earlier: *Not as though I had already attained, either were already perfect: but I follow after, if that I may apprehend that for which also I am apprehended of Christ Jesus* (Philippians 3:12).

Spiritual formation is never accomplished until each of us stands before our Maker. I have no greater desire than to stand before Him someday with my family, my church, and you and to hear these words:

The Conclusion of Spiritual Formation

Well done, thou good and faithful servant: thou hast been faithful over a few things, I will make thee ruler over many things: enter thou into the joy of thy lord (Matthew 25:21).

Lest I Forget

On page six of this book I told you about an unappreciated question from a mentor. Now allow me to bid you farewell by sharing that question. Sitting in a mid-pandemic Zoom meeting, I was asked, "What new thing is God leading you to do in the next season of your ministry?"

If you had forty years of full-time ministry experience under your belt and I asked you this question, you would be set back a bit, too. You would probably obfuscate in the same manner I did. Anyway, how does one share his most intimate communications from God with a near stranger?

I wish I could share the complete answer, but I cannot because it is still being formed in me. Oh, at first I struggled to write three sentences, which now seem quite ambiguous. For the Lord continues to speak in that still, small voice. He continues His forming and shaping process in me. He never stops; He never will. However, I have already shared part of my answer. You have just completed reading it.

The offending question was the genesis of *Formed: A Journey of Spiritual Formation.* Stay tuned; there is more to come.

Thank you for joining me in this journey.

Your humble servant,
R. Kent Smith